The Courage to Teach
Guide for Reflection
and Renewal

Tenth Anniversary Edition

JB JOSSEY-BASS

The Courage to Teach Guide for Reflection and Renewal

Tenth Anniversary Edition

Parker J. Palmer

with Megan Scribner

BICENTENNIAL

1807

WILEY

2007

BICENTENNIAL

John Wiley & Sons

Published by Jossey-Bass
A Wiley Imprint
989 Market Street, San Francisco, CA 94103-1741   www.josseybass.com

Wiley Bicentennial logo: Richard J. Pacifico

Credits are on page 179.

Readers should be aware that Internet Web sites offered as citations and/or sources for further information may have changed or disappeared between the time this was written and when it is read.

Jossey-Bass books and products are available through most bookstores. To contact Jossey-Bass directly call our Customer Care Department within the U.S. at 800-956-7739, outside the U.S. at 317-572-3986, or fax 317-572-4002.

Jossey-Bass also publishes its books in a variety of electronic formats. Some content that appears in print may not be available in electronic books.

Library of Congress Cataloging-in-Publication Data
Palmer, Parker J.
  The courage to teach guide for reflection and renewal / Parker J. Palmer with Megan Scribner. — 10th anniversary ed.
     p. cm.
  ISBN-13: 978-0-7879-9687-1 (pbk.)
  1. Teachers. 2. Teaching. 3. Learning. I. Scribner, Megan. II. Title.
  LB1775.P257 2007
  371.1—dc22   2007020648

Printed in the United States of America
TENTH ANNIVERSARY EDITION
HB Printing   10 9 8 7 6 5 4 3 2 1

Contents

Foreword

When I published *The Courage to Teach* in 1997, I hoped it would contribute to the growing national conversation about reforming education, especially teaching and learning. Over the past decade, that hope has been fulfilled to a greater degree than I ever imagined possible. Now, in 2007, with the publication of an expanded tenth anniversary edition of *The Courage to Teach,* my hope is that the book will continue to contribute to a conversation that has become wider, deeper, and more persuasive than it was a decade ago.

That the book has been a best seller is gratifying, of course. But far more important to me are the messages I receive every week from educators who tell me that *The Courage to Teach* speaks their truth—and that they are acting on some of its ideas. Today, ten years after publication, there is evidence that the book has contributed not just to a conversation but to a movement for education reform, evidence in the form of research, publications, workshops, conferences, and transformed institutional policies and practices. (For some of this evidence, please see the Foreword to the 2007 edition of *The Courage to Teach.*)

The fact that *Courage* has attracted many readers from worlds other than education—including medicine, law, politics, philanthropy, ministry, and organizational leadership—has both gratified and surprised me. And yet, looking back, perhaps I should have expected this. Ever since the book came out, people have asked me, "Why not a book called *The Courage to Lead, The Courage to Serve,* or *The Courage to Heal*? So many insights in *The Courage to Teach* apply to other fields."

Every profession that attracts people for reasons of the heart is one in which people and the work they do suffer from losing heart. These people, like teachers, ask themselves, "How can we take heart again so that we can give heart to others?"—which is why they undertook their work in the first place.

The idea for this *Guide,* whose first edition was published in 1999, came from my friends and colleagues at Jossey-Bass who wanted to support teachers in reclaiming their inner lives and working for education reform. Now—as a companion piece to the tenth anniversary edition of *The Courage to Teach*—the *Guide* has been revised and expanded to serve teachers even better, along with people in other professions who have been drawn to the book's central themes.

Jossey-Bass is a rarity among publishers, with a mission not only to sell books but also to effect positive social change. This *Guide* is a natural outcome of that commitment: it is designed to help individuals and groups explore *The Courage to Teach* and translate its key ideas into meaningful action in their own lives and institutions.

With this revised edition of the *Guide* you will find a DVD that includes a seventy-minute interview with me and a video tour of a retreat program for personal and professional renewal—also called "The Courage to Teach"—that has developed over the past fifteen years. (More information about this program, which is now up and running in some thirty states and fifty cities, will be found in Appendixes D and E. The contents of the DVD are listed on pages 177–178.) We hope that the DVD will make it even easier for people to be in dialogue with the ideas in the book.

Margaret Mead said, "Never doubt that a small group of thoughtful, committed citizens can change the world; indeed, it's the only thing that ever has." I am grateful to the Jossey-Bass staff for understanding those words, for wanting to help people in many lines of work live into their meaning, and for doing the hard work necessary to create this *Guide* and get it into the right hands.

Special thanks go to editor Sheryl Fullerton, production editor Joanne Clapp Fullagar, and two people who are no longer at Jossey-Bass: Carol Brown and the late Sarah Polster. Sarah was the editor who brought me to Jossey-Bass, and I will always cherish her memory. Thanks also to Rachel Livsey, who wrote the first draft of the original *Guide* and provided a solid framework for it; to Judy Brown, Janis Claflin, Debbie DeWitt, Sally Hare, Marianne Houston, Marcy Jackson, Rick Jackson, and Penny Williamson—my friends and colleagues from the Center for Courage & Renewal—for providing materials from their own work with teachers; and to Marcy Jackson, Rick Jackson, Sharon Palmer, and Sarah Polster for their help in editing the first edition of the *Guide*. And thanks to David Leo-Nyquist for his thoughtful reflections on how this revised edition of the *Guide* could help readers understand that the phrase "the courage to teach" now names not only a book but a program for personal and professional renewal and a growing movement for institutional transformation.

Last, but far from least, my heartfelt thanks go to my dear friend and colleague Megan Scribner for helping to create this revised edition of the *Guide* with her typical skill, speed, and *savoir faire*. Without Megan's good work, this *Guide* would not be.

When the *Guide* uses the authorial "we"—as in "We hope you will find this material useful"—the immediate reference is to the people named above. But Marge Piercy has it right in her poem "Low Road" when she says, referring to the growth of a movement, "it starts when you say *We* / and know who you mean, and each / day you mean one more."

We mean you and those who gather with you to engage in truth-telling about teaching, healing, serving, or leading. We mean anyone who cares about doing his or her work in ways that serve other people and our suffering world truly and well.

Madison, Wisconsin   Parker J. Palmer
May 2007

The Courage to Teach
Guide for Reflection
and Renewal

Tenth Anniversary Edition

Introduction

This book is for teachers who have good days and bad,
and whose bad days bring the suffering that comes
only from something one loves. It is for teachers who
refuse to harden their hearts because they
love learners, learning, and the teaching life.

Those words, from the first page of *The Courage to Teach,* also describe the kind of teachers for whom we wrote this *Guide for Reflection and Renewal.* Designed to support both solitary reflection and group dialogue, the *Guide* offers a variety of approaches to "exploring the inner landscape of a teacher's life."

Why embark on an inner journey in the first place? Because teaching, like any truly human activity, emerges from one's inwardness, for better or worse. As I teach, I project the condition of my soul onto my students, my subject, and our way of being together. The entanglements I experience in the classroom are often no more or less than the convolutions of my inner life. Viewed from this angle, teaching holds a mirror to the soul. If I am willing to look in that mirror and not run from what I see, I have a chance to gain self-knowledge—and knowing myself is as crucial to good teaching as knowing my students and my subject.

Of course, this focus on the teacher's inner life is not exactly a conventional approach to problem solving in education! We normally try to resolve educational dilemmas by adopting a new technique or changing the curriculum, not by deepening our own sense of identity and integrity. We focus on the "whats" and the "hows" of teaching— "What subjects shall we teach?" and "What methods shall we use?"—questions that are obviously worth asking.

But rarely, if ever, do we ask the equally important "who" question: "Who is the self that teaches? How does the quality of my selfhood form, or deform, the way I relate to my students, my subject, my colleagues, my world? And how can educational institutions help teachers sustain and deepen the selfhood from which good teaching comes?"

This *Guide,* like the book to which it is kin, invites us to explore the inner landscape of a teacher's life along three distinct but related pathways: intellectual, emotional, and spiritual. By intellectual, I mean the way we think about teaching and learning, about our subjects and our students. By emotional, I mean the way we and our students feel as we teach and learn. By spiritual, I refer to the diverse ways we deal with our eternal longing to be connected with something larger than our own egos.

In *The Courage to Teach,* I wrote, "Intellect, emotion, and spirit depend on one another for wholeness. They are interwoven in the human self and in education at its best, and I have tried to interweave them in this book as well." I have also tried to interweave them in this *Guide for Reflection and Renewal.*

IF YOU ARE NOT a teacher, when you find references in this *Guide* to "teachers" and "teaching" or "learners" and "learning," replace those words with whatever language applies to your profession. The materials in this *Guide*—like many of the insights in *The Courage to Teach* itself—can be translated into any line of work where it is important to connect who you are with what you do, to "rejoin soul and role."

The *Guide* raises questions, examines ideas, explores images, and suggests practices that emerge from the insights offered in *The Courage to Teach*. Because the *Guide* is focused on the teacher's inner life rather than on techniques specific to certain teaching situations, it can be used by teachers at every level and in every setting: university professors, pre-K–12 teachers, community college faculty, adult educators, corporate trainers. Though our society tends to segregate and even rank teachers by "type," the underlying dynamics of teaching cut across these differences, giving teachers of all sorts common struggles and joys.

This edition of the *Guide* includes a DVD of a seventy-minute interview I did to explore various themes related to the book called *The Courage to Teach* and to the retreat program of the same name. (You can read more about the program in Appendixes D and E at the back of this *Guide* and take an audiovisual tour of it on the DVD.) You can view the DVD from start to finish, of course, and use it in any way you see fit for personal reflection or with a book study group. But to make its use a bit easier, scattered throughout this *Guide* are references to particular sections of the DVD that may enhance and enliven your exploration of particular themes from the book.

Part One of this *Guide,* "Guidelines for Individual and Group Study," deals with the process of reflecting on *The Courage to Teach* and with getting ready for that process. Most of the suggestions are about creating "space"—physical, intellectual, emotional, and spiritual space—that is safe and trustworthy, conducive to honest self-exploration as well as corporate inquiry. Whether you are reflecting in solitude or serving as a group facilitator, these suggestions can help create a hospitable context for the work you want to do.

Part Two, "Questions and Activities for Each Chapter," follows the flow of topics in the book, lifting up substantive issues about self and colleagues, students and subjects that can help teachers reflect on their vocation. These questions and activities reach across a wide range of possibilities—from conceptual challenges meant to provoke thought to emotional probes meant to evoke feeling to spiritual queries meant to illumine the foundations of one's life and work. We have tried to design this section to give you a wide range of choices as you seek the approaches that are most appropriate to your own needs or those of your group.

At the back of this *Guide,* we have assembled a variety of resources and background materials that we hope you will find helpful:

- Appendixes A and B contain suggestions and materials to help you plan, design, and organize your *Courage to Teach* book discussion group.

- Appendix C offers a detailed, in-depth description of a discernment process called the clearness committee, which is described in Part One of this *Guide.*

- Appendix D describes the work of the Center for Courage & Renewal and its Courage to Teach retreat program.

- Appendix E describes the theory of personal and institutional transformation that animates and guides the Courage to Teach program.

- Appendix F offers an annotated bibliography for those who want to know more about the many books, articles, and programs related to the book and the Courage to Teach program.

The journey to deepen our understanding of "the teaching self" is long, usually lifelong! Like any journey, it has its difficult passages. But the more familiar we are with our inner terrain, the more sure-footed our teaching—and living—becomes. By taking the inner journey, alone and together, we can contribute to the renewal of our individual vocations, to the reform of education as a whole, and to the well-being of the students we serve.

IN THE DECADE SINCE *The Courage to Teach* was published, the movement toward taking seriously the "inner landscape of a teacher's life" has gained momentum. Helping that movement along has been the Center for Courage & Renewal, founded in 1997 to administer the Courage to Teach program associated with the book.

Working through a network of nearly one hundred fifty trained facilitators, the Center offers programs in thirty states and fifty cities to help people in many walks of life "reconnect who they are with what they do." In facilitated retreat groups called "circles of trust," the Center today works not only with pre-K–12 educators in the public schools but with physicians, lawyers, clergy, foundation executives, politicians, and nonprofit leaders as well. More information about the Center for Courage & Renewal will be found in Appendix D and at the Center's Web site (www.CourageRenewal.org).

This *Guide* is intended to help you conduct the best possible personal or group exploration of *The Courage to Teach* and the accompanying DVD. But it is *not* intended to prepare you to become a facilitator of circles of trust of the sort sponsored by the Center for Courage & Renewal. If you are interested in becoming a facilitator, we suggest that you first read Parker J. Palmer, *A Hidden Wholeness: The Journey Toward an Undivided Life* (Jossey-Bass, 2004). Then—if you want to experience a circle of trust and learn more about the art and craft of facilitation—please visit the Web site of the Center for Courage & Renewal to get information about its facilitator preparation program.

PART ONE

Guidelines for Individual and Group Study

Teaching is a vocation that requires constant renewal of mind, heart, and spirit—if we want to avoid burnout, take joy in our work, and grow in our service to students. As we seek renewal, there are two primary sources to which we can turn: the inner teacher who speaks in solitude, and the community of fellow teachers. The guidelines in Part One are intended to make the resources of both solitude and community more accessible to teachers in quest of renewal.

The issues raised by *The Courage to Teach* require us to practice openness and vulnerability, with ourselves and with each other, virtues that rarely receive their due in professional settings. We need guidelines for reflection and discussion that encourage us to explore our inner landscapes in a deeply respectful way, a way that encourages the soul to come forward and speak its truth.

What follows is not to be read as a manual of techniques for reflection; teaching and learning cannot be reduced to technique. What follows are reminders to walk quietly, remain observant, practice listening, and stay open to discovering the important truths that inhabit the inner landscapes of our lives.

IF YOU ARE NOT a teacher, when you find references in this *Guide* to "teachers" and "teaching" or "learners" and "learning," replace those words with whatever language applies to your profession. The materials in this *Guide*—like many of the insights in *The Courage to Teach* itself—can be translated into any line of work where it is important to connect who you are with what you do, to "rejoin soul and role."

INDIVIDUAL STUDY

If you are studying *The Courage to Teach* solo, you doubtless know how you want to proceed because you know what works for you. But for whatever they may be worth, here are some reminders that may prove useful as you get under way.

Physical space is more important to reflection than we may understand—especially after spending years in educational institutions, which are notoriously insensitive to the impact that physical settings can have on the human spirit!

Try to find a place where you feel comfortable, one that is free from both distractions and interruptions. Some people can go on retreat by closing their office door and turning off the phone. Others need a space where there are no reminders of work to be done. Others need neutral turf where they can "disappear" into anonymity—a public library or a coffee shop. Still others need to be in a natural setting. Find a space that feels hospitable to you, and claim it for yourself.

If you are working through this *Guide* alone, one of your major challenges will be setting aside a scheduled time for reflection—and then holding to it. You may want to choose a regular day each week when you can protect at least an hour or two to reflect on your life as a teacher. Choose a time of day when you are the least likely to face other distractions—perhaps early in the morning before the pace of the workday quickens or late in the evening when your world has slowed a bit.

Once you have chosen a day and time, put it on your calendar and treat it as responsibly as you would treat any other commitment. If we take seriously our commitments to other people—as we would if we had a faculty meeting on the calendar—why not take our commitments to ourselves with equal seriousness?

Try to use your reflective time for just that—reflection rather than preparation for reflection. Prepare by reading the chapter you will be reflecting on a day or two before the time you have set aside to reflect. It might help to take some notes or make a journal entry about your reading as well. Let the material "steep" in your mind and heart before you explore it more intentionally. By preparing before reflecting, you leave more time for genuine "inner journeying," for listening openly to what your inner teacher has to say.

GROUP STUDY

At the heart of *The Courage to Teach* is a pivotal image of teaching: "to teach is to create a space in which the community of truth is practiced." *Truth* is defined as "an eternal conversation about things that matter, conducted with passion and discipline." If you are convening and facilitating a group inquiry into the book, your goal is to prepare a space where the "community of truth" can be practiced around the issues in the book itself. (For suggestions and materials for convening a book discussion group, see Appendixes A and B.)

Membership and Leadership

The idea of community scares some people away because they fear getting caught in something that will add pressure to their lives. So it is important to be clear at the outset about the level of commitment each participant is willing to make to the group and about the proposed duration of the group's life. If some participants desire a long-term group, establish periodic checkout points, times when people can decide to rejoin or leave, guilt-free. Long-term groups will eventually face the question of whether, when, and how new persons may join—a question that requires thoughtful consideration in groups that have worked hard on creating "safe" space with each other.

Community is a dynamic state of affairs that is not anarchic but requires leadership at every turn. While it is possible for a group to hold fruitful sessions without formal leadership—sessions in which participants share such leadership responsibilities as maintaining the boundaries of the space, keeping it open for all to participate, and dealing creatively with conflict—it is often helpful to have one person designated to facilitate the process. This may be the same person each time, or the role may rotate. You might want to discuss this issue as a group and reach consensus on what leadership pattern suits your group's needs.

But whether the leadership role is designated, rotated, or jointly shared, its purpose remains the same: to create a teaching and learning space centered on the great thing called teaching. By giving thoughtful consideration to the shaping of that space—in its physical, intellectual, emotional, and spiritual dimensions—you can help create an environment supportive of reflection and renewal.

Physical Space

If you have a choice of meeting places, ask yourself which one feels most like the space required for a community of truth. If it is possible to meet in a noninstitutional space, such as someone's home, the quality of conversation may deepen considerably. But even if your choice of meeting places is limited, there are simple steps you can take to create a physical space that promotes open and honest dialogue.

Make sure it is a private space on which you can close the door and not be overheard by others, a place where you will not be bothered by telephones ringing or fax machines beeping. Try to arrange for comfortable chairs, warm (nonfluorescent) lighting, fresh air, and a comfortable temperature. Sitting in a circle helps foster good discussion—a circle unbroken by intervening tables or desks so that participants are not barricaded but have a sense of access to one another.

Some of the activities in Part Two involve writing, so remind people to bring notepads or journals. If refreshments are possible, perhaps provided by a different person each time, they can enhance the sense of community. If it suits your style, a lighted candle at the center of the circle will enliven almost any space.

Intellectual Space

A good teaching and learning space is created, in part, by a tension between conceptual boundaries that keep the group focused on a topic and the openness necessary to allow them to explore that topic. Review the chapter you will be dealing with. Which of its concepts constitute the essential boundaries of the topic on which you want to focus? How can you introduce those concepts clearly and compellingly while still leaving room for participants to expand them and bring their own ideas to the table?

Of the questions and activities supplied in Part Two of this *Guide,* which ones seem most appropriate to your group? Which might best serve as preparatory exercises before the session, and which would best be introduced once the session is under way? What questions and activities of your own devising might help the process along? Are there newspaper articles, poems, art, or music that might stimulate ideas in the group?

Think about the participants individually, and ask yourself what they need to be brought into this sort of inquiry. Do they need a chance to reflect silently in a journal before speaking, or would it be better to go directly to discussion? Do they need small-group discussions followed by a large-group dialogue in order to give everyone "airtime," or would large-group discussions suffice? Do the discussions need to be ends in themselves, or would taking minutes and creating some sort of record or report make the work more valuable for some participants?

A safe intellectual space encourages participants to listen and respond respectfully to each other's thoughts so that everyone can express their thoughts openly, without fear of personal put-downs. This does not mean that there can be no disagreement or debate; on the contrary, the safety to engage in creative conflict is a crucial test of good intellectual space. But it does mean that we need to deal with contentious topics in ways that leave no one feeling mistreated.

Though those "ways" have more to do with the spirit of the discussion than with technique, there are methods that can help—if the spirit is right. For example, you might have participants write about the topic you wish to discuss on three-by-five-inch cards, stating their views on the issue and leaving the cards unsigned. Collect the cards, shuffle them, redistribute them to the group, and then ask each person to read aloud what is on his or her card and comment on its content for no more than two minutes. Not knowing whose views one is commenting on tends to make the comments more measured—and an initial go-round of this sort can till the soil for a more open and yet respectful discussion.

These suggestions for creating intellectual space reflect the premise that a good teacher does not fill the space so much as open it up for others. As the facilitator of your book study group, try to ask rather than tell, to explore rather than advocate, to wonder rather than know, to trust that people are thinking and learning in silence as well as in conversation.

But the task of keeping the intellectual space open and safe should not belong to the facilitator alone; it needs to be shared by the group. At the first meeting, invite participants to create a list of ground rules for good dialogue, so that some of the issues we've noted here can be addressed before they arise—rules such as "Make space for everyone to speak" or "State both what you agree with and what you disagree with when you respond to someone." If you use such rules as a checklist, asking the group to assess its own behavior against its own norms at the end of every session, the group will keep itself healthy.

Emotional Space

Exploring our identity and integrity as teachers requires us to tell the truth about our feelings. But it is difficult to overcome conventional norms that reward us for suppressing that truth, for keeping the conversation on the surface of our lives. So while it is important to create a space that is hospitable to ideas, it is equally important to create a space that is hospitable to feelings. Indeed, it is arguably more important, for in a space that is hostile to feelings, it is unlikely that either intellectual or emotional truth will emerge.

As the facilitator of your book study group, you can help foster emotional hospitality by listening attentively, asking good questions, offering supportive words, and practicing a nonjudgmental attitude. If the emotional space is being shut down by harsh responses to others' ideas, remind people that it is possible to speak for ourselves without speaking against others.

Try to ensure that everyone in the group has a chance to participate. For example, create a ground rule that no one can speak more than five or six times in a given hour. If that feels too mechanical, stay alert to how many people have spoken, and if a few are dominating the dialogue while others are silenced, wait for a pause and say, "For the next little while, let's make space for those who'd like to speak but have not yet had a chance to do so."

Creating an atmosphere of dignity and regard for each participant is, of course, crucial. People are more likely to be open with each other if they know their voices will be heard and their contributions respected. An indirect way of establishing that ethos is to invite people to introduce themselves anew at each session via a meaningful but nonthreatening question: "Tell us about an older person who has been important in your life" or "Tell us about a powerful learning experience you've had, in or out of school." It is a simple fact that the more one knows about another person's story, the less possible it is to dismiss or disrespect that person.

To encourage emotional honesty, it is essential that participants commit themselves to confidentiality. In fact, in the retreat program called the Courage to Teach, we ask participants to honor a rule of "double confidentiality": nothing said in the group will be repeated outside the group, and members are not free to approach each other after group sessions (to clarify a point or offer advice, for example) unless they are invited to do so. The assurance that one will not be pursued, cornered, and counseled after a gathering makes it easier to speak one's truth.

Spiritual Space

A spiritual space is one in which the inner teacher can speak its truth and have a chance to be heard. How do we create such a space? By learning not to invade each other's solitude in a vain and alienating effort to advise, save, or fix each other up but instead learning to practice simple receptivity and listening of the sort that allows people to listen more deeply to themselves.

In our culture, the approved response when we hear almost any sort of problem is to offer advice that will "fix the problem." Unfortunately, this reflexive fix-it response often makes the person who shared the problem feel unheard and dismissed. Indeed, our tendency to offer fixes stems from the desire to distance ourselves from the person with a problem: if you take my advice, you will be fine, and I don't need to worry about you anymore; if you don't take my advice, I have done the best I could, and I can forget about you and your dilemma.

The soul doesn't want to be fixed; in fact, it flees and hides when pursued by a "fixer." The soul wants only to be welcomed, attended to, and heard by people who are willing to offer it simple hospitality. You can help make this possible by instituting and enforcing a group norm against trying to fix each other. Be clear with group participants that unless someone specifically asks for advice, you are not gathered to solve each other's problems but to "hear each other into speech," to cultivate seeds of possibility in each other's lives without worrying about whether or how or when those seeds will grow.

There is a simple behavior that can help us avoid our tendency to try to fix each other: we can learn to ask honest, open questions instead of giving gratuitous analyses or advice.

An honest, open question is one that I ask you without believing that I know the "right" answer and without hoping that you will give me the answer I have in mind. If, for example, I ask you, "Have you ever considered seeing a therapist?" it is probably not an honest, open question. In all likelihood, the question reflects my belief that you should see a therapist, and even as I ask it, I am probably hoping that you will agree.

An honest, open question might be, "Has anything like this ever happened to you before?" If so, "What helped you deal with that situation?" "Are there insights from that experience that might be helpful to you now?" With questions such as these, it would be hard for me to have a "right" answer in mind and to be hoping that you will give me that answer. The motive behind questions such as these is to help you reflect on yourself rather than to convince you to see things my way or any other particular way.

Asking honest, open questions is obviously not the only useful or acceptable form of group discourse. There is always a place for sharing information, for respectful disagreement, for creative conflict over ideas. But honest, open questioning is a discipline that can help your group at those vulnerable points where community tends to self-destruct—and to shut down the voice of the inner teacher—by becoming invasive rather than supportive of the soul.

There is one more group discipline that can open space for the soul to speak its truth, one that can be especially useful as a postlude, or even prelude, to a difficult conversation. Gather the group in a circle and settle into silence. Tell them that they are free to speak out of the silence whenever they wish—to speak from their own center to the center of the circle—but are forbidden to respond directly to another person. Everyone is free to speak his or her truth, but no one is free to comment on what another person says. Given this protection, people feel free to share fragile insights or struggles that might not be voiced if they thought they were going to be rebutted, corrected, or even affirmed. Under these conditions, we learn to give the soul the deep listening and receptivity that it wants and needs.

15

Six Paradoxes of Space

As you think about creating the various forms of nonphysical "space" that will help your group do its work, you might want to recall the six paradoxical tensions of pedagogical space named in *The Courage to Teach* and use them as a checklist:

- The space should be bounded and open.
- The space should be hospitable and "charged."
- The space should invite the voice of the individual and the voice of the group.
- The space should honor the "little" stories of the participants and the "big" stories of teaching, learning, identity, and integrity.
- The space should support solitude and surround it with the resources of the community.
- The space should welcome both silence and speech.

Indeed, you might want to review the book's full discussion of these paradoxes (see *The Courage to Teach,* pp. 76–80) as you prepare to gather your group. You will find there clues for the creation of the kind of intellectual, emotional, and spiritual space that invites and encourages the "community of truth."

The Clearness Committee

The clearness committee is a specialized and demanding process of discernment that is neither necessary nor appropriate for every individual or every group. However, if someone in your group is struggling with a particularly difficult issue and, after thoughtful consideration, feels that this might be helpful in the search for inner guidance, you might want to offer your group the opportunity—in fact, the privilege—of participating in a clearness committee.

Rightly done (and it is critical that it be rightly done, because it invites people to make themselves vulnerable and promises that they will not be exploited in the process), the clearness committee teaches us how to help each other with problems while avoiding the arrogance of believing we can "save" or "fix" each other. It offers a deep experience of a form of community in which we neither invade each other's integrity nor evade each other's struggles. Many people report that the experience has led to significant changes in their personal and professional lives.

An overview of the clearness committee is found in *The Courage to Teach* (pp. 157–161). But if you wish to use this process, it is important that you spend time with Appendix C of this *Guide*. There you will find vital, step-by-step guidance for holding a clearness committee, whose principles and practices you need to study, understand, and embrace before offering the process to others—who themselves need to study, understand, and embrace the principles and practices that make this approach the extraordinary experience it is.

Touchstones for Creating Safe Spaces

The following "touchstones" were created by the Center for Courage & Renewal as guides for creating the safe spaces that we call "circles of trust." (See Appendixes D and E for further information about the Center and its retreat programs.) Keeping these touchstones in mind and sharing them with your participants can be helpful as you plan and lead your *Courage to Teach* book discussions.*

- *Extend and receive welcome.* People learn best in hospitable spaces. In this circle, we support each other's learning by giving and receiving hospitality.
- *Be present as fully as possible.* Be here with your doubts, fears, and failings as well as your convictions, joys, and successes, your listening as well as your speaking.

---

* The first version of this list was developed by Judy Brown, a Courage & Renewal facilitator, in 1994. Her original list of five items has been expanded through the contributions of other facilitators during the past decade. This version, edited and revised by Marcy Jackson and Parker J. Palmer in August 2006, incorporates many of those contributions.

- *What is offered in the circle is by invitation, not demand.* This is not a "share or die" event! During this retreat, do whatever your soul calls for, and know that you do it with our support. Your soul knows your needs better than we do.

- *Speak your truth in ways that respect other people's truth.* Our views of reality may differ, but speaking one's truth in a circle of trust does not mean interpreting, correcting, or debating what others say. Speak from your center to the center of the circle, using "I" statements, trusting people to do their own sifting and winnowing.

- *No fixing, no saving, no advising, and no setting each other straight.* This is one of the hardest guidelines to follow for those of us in the helping professions. But it is vital to welcoming the soul, to making space for the inner teacher.

- *Learn to respond to others with honest, open questions* instead of counsel, corrections, and the like. With such questions, we help "hear each other into deeper speech."

- *When the going gets rough, turn to wonder.* If you feel judgmental or defensive, ask yourself, "I wonder what brought her to this belief?" "I wonder what he's feeling right now?" "I wonder what my reaction teaches me about myself?" Set aside judgment to listen to others—and to yourself—more deeply.

- *Attend to your own inner teacher.* We learn from others, of course. But as we explore poems, stories, questions, and silence in a circle of trust, we have a special opportunity to learn from within. So pay close attention to your own reactions and responses, to your most important teacher.

- *Trust and learn from the silence.* Silence is a gift in our noisy world and a way of knowing in itself. Treat silence as a member of the group. After someone has spoken, take time to reflect without immediately filling the space with words.

- *Observe deep confidentiality.* Nothing said in a circle of trust will ever be repeated to other people.

- *Know you can get what you need.* Participate with the knowledge that it is possible to leave the circle with whatever it was you needed when you arrived and that the seeds planted here can keep growing in the days ahead.

A WORD OF ENCOURAGEMENT

We hope that these guidelines will help you create the physical, emotional, intellectual, and spiritual space to encourage deep reflection and real renewal. We know that this work is not easily done. But we also know that when teachers are able to come together in a space that has these qualities, the benefits for us as persons and as professionals are considerable—and the ultimate beneficiaries are the students we are committed to serving.

PART TWO

Questions and Activities for Each Chapter

I n Part Two, we walk slowly through *The Courage to Teach,* one chapter at a time. Key themes in each chapter are highlighted, each followed by a set of questions and activities whose intent is to stimulate both individual and group reflection.

The same intent lies behind the DVD that accompanies this *Guide.* The DVD—which can be viewed in its entirety or in any of its twenty-four segments, each about three minutes in length—features an extensive interview in which I was asked to think out loud about some of the central ideas I explored in *The Courage to Teach.*

Throughout this part of the *Guide,* we connect particular segments of the DVD to key themes in a chapter and offer questions to focus a discussion of those parts of the interview. These "DVD questions" can be used interchangeably with the "book questions" to deepen your exploration of either the interview or the text.

You may find it helpful to use a brief segment or two of the DVD to jump-start your book discussions, since hearing and seeing the interview has an immediacy that a book, read several days ago, does not. But because the book examines nuances that cannot be addressed in an interview, impress your participants with the importance of doing their homework—just as they try to impress their students!

If you are studying the book solo, we suggest that you focus on just a few questions, scanning to find the ones that speak most deeply to you. You might want to respond to them in writing as if you were keeping a journal.

IF YOU ARE NOT a teacher, when you find references in this *Guide* to "teachers" and "teaching" or "learners" and "learning," replace those words with whatever language applies to your profession. The materials in this *Guide*—like many of the insights in *The Courage to Teach* itself—can be translated into any line of work where it is important to connect who you are with what you do, to "rejoin soul and role."

If you are leading a group, do not feel pressed to "cover the field" by trying to use all of the two hundred or so questions that follow. For each session, choose a key question or cluster of questions on a particular topic, keeping a few others in reserve in case the discussion gets stuck. You may also want to develop your own questions and activities, perhaps inviting others in your group to share in that process.

Remember that these questions can be used not only to guide large- and small-group explorations but also to focus silent reflection and journaling prior to group dialogue. Using them for such purposes will help keep the inquiry slow and gentle and thus help it go deep. The "inner work" invited by *The Courage to Teach* cannot be rushed; it requires a generosity of time.

Chapter I

The Heart of a Teacher
Identity and Integrity in Teaching

A. *If we want to grow as teachers, we must learn to talk to each other about our inner lives, our own identity and integrity.*

1. As you study this book with others, you are invited to share your strengths and your weaknesses, your hopes and your despairs—or to confront them on your own. What are your expectations for this process? What fears do you have about it? How are you encouraged or discouraged in such sharing by the institution in which you teach?

2. Write journal responses to these questions and, if appropriate, share them: What drew you to participate in this inquiry? What do you want others to know about your strengths and weaknesses and about your learning style that would help you participate fully in this group? What do you want to recall about yourself as you engage in solitary reflection?

3. Write a personal statement trying to express what is at the heart of your life as a teacher. Consider the following questions: Why did I become a teacher? What do I stand for as a teacher? What are the "birthright gifts" that I bring to my lifework? What do I want my legacy as a teacher to be? What can I do to "keep track of myself," to remember my own heart?

 SEGMENT 1: EDUCATING THE HEART

- What are your inner gifts, the gifts you bring to the world simply by being who you are?
- Do you feel able to give your gifts freely? If not, what is keeping you from doing so?
- How do you understand the phrase "the education of the heart" and its implications for teaching and learning?
- What experiences have you had at trying to educate the "heart that moves the hand" as well as the mind whose cognitive capacities the skillful hand requires?

THE COURAGE TO TEACH GUIDE FOR REFLECTION AND RENEWAL

B. Identity lies in the intersection of the diverse forces that make up a life, while integrity lies in relating to those forces in ways that bring us wholeness and life.

4. Identity and integrity are closely related concepts. How do you understand their relationships and distinctions? What does each concept mean to you?

5. Do you have a story about a teacher whose work clearly flows from identity and integrity? About a teacher who seemed to be out of touch with his or her identity? What insights do you draw from these stories?

6. When did you first know that you wanted to become a teacher? Do you have childhood memories or stories that seem to connect with your adult decision to pursue this vocation? Share your responses, listening carefully for the "seeds of vocation" in your own life and others' lives.

7. When did you first realize that you *are* a teacher? What were the circumstances of this realization? What feelings accompanied it? How close are you to those feelings today?

 SEGMENT 2: TEACHING WITH PASSION

- In relation to your work, what are you most passionate about?
- To what extent are your passions integral to who you are, such that you would feel diminished if you were unable to express them?
- Does the subject you teach give you a "richer view of the world and a larger sense of self"? In what ways? Has that aspect of your work changed over time?
- How do you engage students in your passion for your subject in a way that does not ignore their passions and at the same time gives them an opportunity to grow into new ones?

C. Good teaching cannot be reduced to technique; good teaching comes from the identity and integrity of the teacher.

    8. What aspects of your identity and integrity feel most supported by and engaged with the work you do? What aspects of your identity and integrity feel most threatened or endangered by your work?

    9. As a teacher, are there moments when you have attempted to protect your identity and integrity from being violated? Are there other moments when you have allowed some sort of violation to occur?

    10. "Good teachers possess a capacity for connectedness." They "weave" the connections between themselves, their subjects, and their students on "the loom of the heart." How does that image speak to you? What is your experience of trying to hold the tension of these connections in your heart?

    11. "The undivided self" is one in which every major thread of one's life experience is honored, creating a weave of such coherence and strength that it can hold together students, subject, and self. Do you know anyone, in any field, who seems to have an undivided self? How does that quality manifest itself in the work that person does?

D. *Bad teachers distance themselves from their students and subjects, while good teachers "join self and subject and students in the fabric of life" (p. 11).*

12. Jane Tompkins discovered that her goal as a teacher had been to put on a "performance," thus distancing herself from students and subject. Do you identify with her self-criticism? If so, do you share Tompkins's diagnosis of fear as the driving force behind this distancing? In what ways other than "performance" do teachers set themselves apart?

13. "The ability to connect with my students and to connect them with the subject depends less on the methods I use than on the degree to which I know and trust my selfhood and make my selfhood available and vulnerable." What does it mean to rely on your selfhood rather than methods? What fears do you have about making your selfhood available and vulnerable? In what ways have these fears led you to disconnect from your students or your subject?

14. What methods have you used to try to connect your students with your subjects? Which ones were effective? Which ones were ineffective? What do you learn about your identity and integrity as a teacher from knowing which methods do and do not work for you?

SEGMENT 3: STUDENTS KNOW

- Think back to a positive teacher-related academic learning experience in your life. How would you describe that teacher as a person? How did that teacher connect with you? How did you connect with that teacher?
- Now think about a teacher from whom you did not learn much. How would you describe that teacher as a person? What went on inside of you in the presence of that teacher?
- What does it feel like when you are connected to your subject? To your students?
- What do you think happens in and among your students when you teach from that place of connection? What happens to your students when that connection is missing?

E. *If we want to deepen our understanding of our integrity, we must experiment with our lives.*

15. What "experiments" have you conducted with your own life? What risks have you taken with these experiments, and what price have you paid? What have you learned from these experiments—about yourself and about the world?

16. What are some ways that teachers may "experiment" with their work in order to deepen their understanding of their own identity and integrity? What can we learn from these experiments in teaching? What are the risks? What are the rewards?

17. Given the balance of risks and rewards, is experimentation—with one's work or one's life—worth it? If so, what is the next experiment you might want to make? Why?

SEGMENT 4: RECLAIMING PASSION

- When did you first know you wanted to be a teacher? How did you know? How did it feel? Do you have a story to tell about a particular moment of self-discovery, or did it come to you more gradually over time?
- As you think back on your original motivation or inspiration to become a teacher, what feelings are evoked in you at this moment? What is the current state of your original desire or passion to teach?
- If you are feeling any sort of pain in relation to your vocation as a teacher, how do you name that pain? How do you understand its source? How do you or might you deal with it?
- If you feel like your "flame" for teaching is flickering or dying or dead, do you want to keep it alive? If so, what would help?
- What is your soul "trying to call forth in you"?

THE COURAGE TO TEACH GUIDE FOR REFLECTION AND RENEWAL

F. *The best gift we receive from great mentors is not their knowledge or their approach to teaching but the sense of self they evoke within us.*

18. Share a story about one of your favorite teachers. What do you most vividly remember about that teacher? How did he or she make you feel? What was his or her relation to the subject taught? What was the ethos of his or her classroom? What does that scenario tell you about that teacher's identity and integrity?

19. Thinking about that same teacher, what does his or her story tell you about who you were at that time in your life? What was it about you, and about that moment in your life, that made this teacher great for you? What gift or truth about yourself did that teacher help reveal?

20. Have you been mentored by someone whose relation to you at the time seemed negative—someone who helped you understand your weaknesses rather than your strengths, your limits rather than your potentials? If so, talk about this relationship and what you got out of it, contrasting your feelings at the time with the feelings you have now.

 SEGMENT 5: THE STORY OF MR. PORTER

- Have you known or heard about a teacher like Mr. Porter "who lifted the life" of a child? If so, tell that story and reflect on it.
- In ways small or large, have you ever experienced being a "Mr. Porter" for one of your students? If so, tell that story and reflect on how it felt.
- At a time when many teachers feel pressured to "teach to the test" rather than teach the child, what can help teachers find the courage to perceive and support "something that no one else had seen" in a child, even if it is not "test-relevant"?
- How can we persuade politicians and others who have power over education that teachers must be able to look beyond the test to see "the child and the child's gifts"? If we cannot persuade them, how can we resist them?

G. *Many of us felt called to teach when we encountered a particular subject or field of study. By recalling how those early encounters evoked a sense of self that was only dormant in us at the time, we may recover the heart to teach.*

21. Reflect on your earliest encounters with the field in which you teach. When did you first feel drawn to it? What was it that drew you? What within you was evoked by this field— its values, its methods, the way it names and frames reality? What does the nature of this field reveal about who you are?

22. If you had a chance to start over, would you stay with the subject you teach or choose a different one? Why? What does your answer tell you about who you are and who you have become?

 SEGMENT 6: MAKING CONNECTIONS

On the DVD, spirituality is defined as "the desire to be connected with something larger than my own ego." In teaching, this translates to "a desire to be connected with my students, the lives they lead, and the subject I am teaching."

- If this definition of spirituality makes sense to you, how would you name your own spirituality as a person?
- As a teacher, what forms of "connectedness" do you experience with some regularity?
- What other forms would you like to experience more often, and what might help that happen?

On the DVD, the claim is made that learning results when you are able to honor your subject "as if it was a person, giving it as much status, standing, and dignity."

- Does this make sense to you?
- If so, what has been your experience at trying to present your subject in this way?
- Can you imagine ways that your capacity for this sort of teaching might be strengthened?

H. The inner teacher acts as a guard at the gate of our selfhood, warding off what insults our integrity and welcoming whatever affirms it.

23. The "inner teacher" is not the same as the "conscience" that speaks exclusively of "oughts" and "ought nots." Is this a useful distinction for you? If so, tell a story that illustrates the difference between the two. If not, why?

24. If you think of yourself as having an inner teacher, how do you try to listen to that voice? What encourages you to do so? What impedes you from doing so?

25. Is there any recent message or clue from your inner teacher that you feel a need to take seriously? If so, what is it, and what do you think it requires of you?

 SEGMENT 7: THE INNER TEACHER

- Do you have space in your daily life for "taking the time to listen to your heart, to let the world get quiet"? If so, how do you create that space? If not, what might you do to create it?
- Do you have experiences of listening for, hearing, and having to deal with "the voice of the inner teacher"? If so, can you tell a story or two about those moments—about how they have felt and what they have meant in your life?
- Because we so easily get lost on the inner journey, we need a community to help us discern what we think we are learning from within. Do you have such a community? If so, what does it do for you? If not, how might you might join or create one?

Chapter II

A Culture of Fear
Education and the Disconnected Life

A. *Fear is a powerful feature of both academic culture and our inner landscape—the fear of having a live encounter with "otherness" in a student, a colleague, a subject, or the voice of the inner teacher.*

1. What are some of your fears in the classroom? In relation to colleagues? In relation to your professional career? How have you dealt with them? What have you learned about yourself and about fear as a result?

2. "Academic institutions offer myriad ways to protect ourselves from a live encounter." Share some of the common ways that teachers protect themselves from a live encounter with their students or with their colleagues or with ideas.

3. What structures at your institution promote a sense of disconnection from students, parents, colleagues, and the administration? What keeps us beholden to these structures?

4. How large a role does fear play in your students' lives? What tactics do students use to avoid live encounters with their teachers? With challenging subjects? How can teachers help students be less fearful?

 SEGMENT 8: EDUCATION IN CRISIS

- What is your response to the claim that the crisis in education is not fundamentally about funding or system problems or kids who can't pass tests but about the "failure to support the people who are doing the work at the deepest levels of their lives"?
- Have you sought support for your needs as a teacher within your institution? Have you found what you were looking for there? Where else might you look?
- How can teachers create "hospitable spaces" where students who are anxious about life can feel safe and do deeper learning? What would help teachers "enlarge and deepen their hearts" for the sake of hospitality toward the young?

B. *Certain fears can be healthy for teachers and students by helping us survive, learn, and grow.*

5. How do you distinguish between healthy fears and pathological fears? What is the balance of those two kinds of fear in our schools?

6. What sorts of fear are healthy for our students? Are those same fears healthy for ourselves? If they are healthy, can they be used more fully in the educational process? Should we do so? Why or why not?

**SEGMENT 9: FEAR AND COURAGE
IN TEACHING**

- In your work setting, is fear used as a "motivator" for you or for your students? If so, what are the consequences? If you see the consequences as negative, how might the "fear strategy" be counteracted to avoid "paralysis of the spirit and mind" for students or teachers?
- What is the teacher's role in creating an "alternative reality" to the school system and the world—a reality that values both teachers' and students' hearts and minds and at the same time allows them to function in the world as it is?
- Have you found it true that one often teaches with "trembling knees"? How can teachers deal with their own fear of inadequacy in the face of the challenges of teaching?
- What sources of courage can teachers tap to "stand with integrity" in an educational system that too often fails to support the hearts of people doing the work?

C. *The way we diagnose our students' condition will determine the pedagogical "prescription" we offer. Rather than rely on stereotypical interpretations of student behavior, we need to understand their marginality and decode the fear that often drives their lives.*

7. As a student, what were your greatest fears? Now think about today's students. How do you compare their life situations to yours at a similar age? What are their fears, and how do they deal with them? How might you address their fears more effectively?

8. Think about the kinds of negative student behaviors that you experience in your classroom. Are there diagnoses of those behaviors that make more sense to you than the "fear" hypothesis? If so, what are they—and what pedagogical "prescription" do your diagnoses suggest?

9. Recall the story of the "student from hell" and the learning that flowed from that experience. If you have had a similar encounter, reflect on it. What did you learn about that student and about yourself? If you feel that you did not learn much, can you imagine ways of returning to that experience in imagination—or to that individual in person—in order to deepen your learning?

10. Make three columns on a sheet of paper. Head the first column "Negative Images of Today's Students," the second column "Fears Faced by Young People in Today's Society," and the third column "Positive Traits of Today's Students." Then fill in the table with observations from your own experience. How do these lists relate? How might this profile inform your teaching?

**SEGMENT 10: THE EMOTIONAL LIFE
OF CHILDREN**

- What is the cost of emphasizing facts and theories while ignoring feelings in teaching and learning? How can teachers bring emotions more fully and consciously into the educational equation?
- What is gained when feelings are honored in the classroom? What is lost or at risk of being lost, and how can teachers deal with these issues?
- Have you experienced moments or long passages of time when rampant fear has "completely shut down" students' minds so that they can't learn? How can teachers help alleviate such debilitating fear?
- How can teachers create safe spaces in which young people feel "hospitably received" so they can learn?
- How can teachers create safe spaces for themselves to care for their own emotional, spiritual, and relational lives? How do you do this for yourself?

D. *Instead of fearing "the judgment of the young" and choosing "stagnation" as a form of self-protection, we can choose "generativity," understood as "creativity in the service of the young."*

11. Do you experience this fear of "the judgment of the young"? If so, what is the root of that fear in you, and how does it manifest itself in your teaching?

12. Have you known an older person who chose generativity over stagnation? How did that choice manifest itself? Do you feel a need to embrace generativity more fully? How might your teaching change if you did so?

13. "Good teaching is an act of hospitality toward the young, and hospitality is always an act that benefits the host even more than the guest." In what specific ways are you hospitable to students? In what ways do you treat them as unwelcome guests? How do teachers benefit from practicing hospitality toward students?

14. Nelle Morton has written about the need to "hear people into speech," especially young people. Did anyone "hear you into speech" when you were young? If so, how did the person do it? How did you benefit from that gift? How can you hand the gift along to your own students?

SEGMENT 11: GOOD TEACHING IS NOT JUST TECHNIQUE

- In your experience and understanding, what is at the heart of good teaching?
- As a teacher, what is your experience of doing your work in a "complex field of forces and continually and generously offering hospitality, safety, and challenge"? How does it feel to stand there, and what does it take to teach from such a place?
- What is it that makes students so fearful? What can you do as a teacher to help them cultivate the courage to learn?

E. *Knowing is always communal. Through knowing, we make community with "the unavailable other," with realities that would elude us without the connective tissue of knowledge. Knowing is a human way to seek relationship, to have encounters and exchanges that will alter us.*

15. Our understanding of how we *know* helps shape how we *teach.* Do you agree that "knowing is always communal"? Why or why not? What are the pedagogical implications of accepting or rejecting this image?

16. What realities in the world are you related to as a result of your knowledge, without which your life would be poorer—realities such as an ecosystem, a period in history, the psychodynamics of human behavior, or the works of Shakespeare? What does it mean to say that such realities are part of the "community" that you inhabit?

17. Describe, as best you can, the sense of community your students possess. How would you like to alter or enlarge the community of your students' lives through the subject that you teach? What would they gain from this expanded sense of community?

18. Evelyn Fox Keller says of Nobel Prize winner Barbara McClintock that her knowing came from "the highest form of love, love that allows for intimacy without the annihilation of difference." Does this kind of love have a place in education? If not, why not? If so, how might it be taught? How might it make a difference if we could teach students to love the world in this way?

SEGMENT 12: WAYS OF KNOWING

- How might you bring the kind of "whole-self" teaching and learning that often takes place in kindergarten into your classroom, even if it is full of undergraduate, graduate, or older adult students?
- How can you create conditions in your classroom that help your students feel comfortable bringing their emotions as well as their intellects into the teaching and learning equation?
- How does one create relational or communal learning situations in a classroom context? What can you do to encourage students to interact with each other, the subject, and teacher in the quest to learn?

F. Fear is fundamental to the human condition and to academic culture. We will always have *our fears—but we do not need to be* our fears.

19. Does the distinction between "having fear" and "being fear" make sense to you experientially? If so, tell a story that illustrates the distinction as you experience it.

20. Tell about a fear, not necessarily related to teaching, that once controlled you but no longer does. What caused you to confront that fear? What helped you get loose from it? What were the results? What did you learn?

21. Spirituality and the religious traditions are, at bottom, about living in the face of fear, at least according to some interpretations. Do you stand in a religious or spiritual tradition that helps you deal with fear? If so, how would you describe it? Alternatively, reflect on your own way of dealing with fear. How would you describe that way? Could it be called your spirituality?

Chapter III

The Hidden Wholeness

Paradox in Teaching and Learning

A. *We are trained to "think the world apart," dissecting it into either-or choices. But we need to learn how to "think the world together," embracing opposites and appreciating paradoxes.*

1. Is there an example from your own subject or discipline of "thinking the world apart," of analyzing the world into pieces and losing an integrative view of reality?

2. "The opposite of a true statement is a false statement, but the opposite of a profound truth can be another profound truth," Niels Bohr observed. Can you name a profound truth in your own life whose "opposite" is equally true for you? How does education normally deal with truths of this sort?

3. List some polarities that dominate our thinking about education (for example, teacher–student, individual–group, facts–feelings, faculty–administration, school–home). Choose one pair, and identify (a) the reasons this polarity is so compelling, (b) the price we pay for holding to it, (c) alternative ways of framing the issue in question that might bridge the so-called opposites, and (d) the benefits of doing so.

4. What paradoxes in teaching are the most difficult for you to hold in creative tension (for example, subjective–objective, true–false, emotion–intellect)? What are the sources of this difficulty within you? What are the sources of this difficulty within the structures of education?

B. *The self is paradoxical: for every gift or strength we possess, there is a corresponding weakness or liability.*

5. Describe, in writing, a moment in teaching when things went so well you knew you were "born to teach." In groups of three, take turns sharing these case studies and help each other name the gifts of the teacher that helped make this good moment possible—not the techniques the teacher used or the moves he or she made but the qualities of the person.

6. Now describe a moment in teaching when things went so poorly you wished you had never been born! In the same groups of three, take turns sharing your case studies and help each other see the limitations and liabilities that are on the flip side of our gifts. (Remember, your purpose is not to prescribe "fixes" for pedagogical problems but to help each other develop deeper understanding of the paradoxes of the self.)

7. Name some of your key gifts or strengths as a teacher. Now name a struggle or difficulty you commonly have in teaching. How do you understand the relation between your profile of giftedness and the kind of trouble you typically get into in the classroom?

8. Imagine a classroom situation in which you start to get into trouble but become aware of this fact while there is still time to do something about it. At this moment, what might it look like to "live more gracefully with your limits"? What can you imagine yourself doing, inwardly and outwardly, that would invoke or reflect this grace?

C. *The principle of paradox can guide us in thinking about classroom dynamics—and in designing a teaching and learning space that can hold the community of truth.*

9. Look back at the discussion of six paradoxes of pedagogical design (pp. 76–80). Choose one to focus on. Share examples of teaching environments you've experienced where this paradox is honored. Have you ever been in a classroom where only half of the paradox was honored while the other half was ignored? Describe what that classroom was like.

10. Again, choose one of the six paradoxes to focus on. Describe ways in which you have tried to hold this paradox in your own teaching. What are the problems involved in holding the tension of this paradox? What are the rewards? What are some additional ways in which it might inform your teaching?

11. When I (Parker Palmer) discuss my first case study—a good moment in my teaching—I describe in some detail what I did outwardly to hold the six paradoxes and how it felt inwardly as I did so (pp. 80–86). Take your own first case, and describe it in similar, step-by-step detail, outwardly and inwardly. Doing so may help you see things about your own pedagogy that would remain invisible without such microscopic examination.

D. *The principle of paradox will not permeate our teaching until we understand that suffering the tensions of opposites is neither to be avoided nor merely survived but must be actively embraced for the way it can expand our hearts.*

12. In what ways have you experienced "suffering" as a teacher? Has your suffering had any redemptive quality to it; has it made your heart larger? What would help you deepen the redemptive quality of the suffering you experience in your work?

13. What happens to you, to your students, and to the ethos of your classroom when you try to avoid the tension of opposites in order to avoid the suffering that tension can bring?

14. To paraphrase E. F. Schumacher (p. 87), "It is only with the help of higher forces—love, beauty, goodness, truth—that the opposites can be reconciled in the living situation." As you try to hold the tension of opposites in your classroom, do you ever feel the forces that Schumacher names? If so, is it your experience that holding the tension somehow "provokes the supply" of these forces?

 SEGMENT 13: TEACHERS ARE CULTURE HEROES

- What kinds of problems are teachers asked to deal with in our society, either directly or indirectly? What kinds of social problems show up in our schools either overtly or covertly that teachers must contend with?
- How do you assess the conditions under which teachers are asked to do their work, especially conditions that bear on the likelihood that their work can be successful and sustainable?
- How do you assess the state of public or political understanding of the teacher's role in our society? If you find it distorted, how do you think it might be changed?
- How do you assess both the status and the morale of the teacher in twenty-first-century America?
- Given all of this, and comparing teachers to other critical professions, do you agree or disagree that "teachers are among our culture heroes"?

E. *Rainer Maria Rilke wrote, "Be patient toward all that is unsolved in your heart and try to love the questions themselves. . . . Do not now seek the answers, which cannot be given you because you would not be able to live them. And the point is, to live everything. Live the questions now. Perhaps you will then gradually, without noticing it, live along some distant day into the answer."*

15. What do these words mean to you? Is there a situation in your life at this moment where you must "live and love the questions" rather than seek the answers? If so, what is frustrating about this way of living? What is liberating about it?

16. What questions are you living at this stage of your life— from "How can I get up in the morning?" to "How can I get a raise?" to "How can I become a better teacher?" to "How can I witness to truth?" Are the questions you are now living the ones you want to live? If not, what questions would you like to be living? How might you hold these questions at the center of your attention?

17. How would teaching and learning be different if, in addition to posing questions with answers that our students need to know, we helped them find questions that are worth living— even though they have no "answers" in any conventional sense?

 SEGMENT 14: WE TEACH WHO WE ARE

- As you think back on your schooling, who were the teachers who connected with you and helped you connect with learning? What was their secret?
- As you think about it *not* from a sociological standpoint but from within your own experience, how do you understand the role and importance of the teacher in our lives?
- What does the proposition "we teach who we are" mean to you? Does it ring true for you? How do you know when you are or are not teaching from "who you are"?
- What happens in those moments when teachers and students connect at a level where "deep speaks to deep"? How can we create more of those moments and connections?

THE COURAGE TO TEACH GUIDE FOR REFLECTION AND RENEWAL

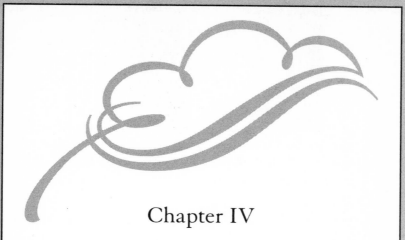

Chapter IV

Knowing in Community
Joined by the Grace of Great Things

A. *Before exploring the issues of educational community considered in this chapter, it might be helpful to explore the experiences and assumptions that members of your group bring to the concept of community itself.*

1. In small groups, talk about an experience of community, of any duration, that has been meaningful to you (letting "community" mean whatever it may mean to each individual). What went on in that situation that made it "community" for you? What was going on in you at that time that made you available to this community?

2. As you listen to each other's stories, make a list of the marks of community, features of certain moments in life that cause us to say, "This is what community is all about." See if you can create a consensus profile of the marks of community. Which of those marks are present, or potentially present, in the setting where you teach?

3. We know that "community," like everything else that is human, can take both healthy and pathological forms. Talk about your experience of the two forms of community, if any. What makes the difference between the two?

B. *At least three models of community can be found in contemporary discourse about the subject—the therapeutic, the civic, and the marketing models (pp. 92–97).*

4. Do you have experience, at school or elsewhere, with any of those three types of community? If so, respond to the analysis of the strengths and weaknesses of that model in light of your own experience.

5. Do you agree that many people in our society are seeking community in their lives? If so, what do you think is behind that yearning? What are the positive and negative potentials in that yearning? What forms of life together are people finding to meet those needs?

6. Is "community" necessary to support the educational mission as you understand it? If so, how does educational community differ, if at all, from the community we seek in other dimensions of our lives?

C. Community is an outward and visible sign of an inward and invisible grace, the flowing of personal identity and integrity into the world of relationships. Only as we are in community with ourselves can we find community with others.

7. What does it mean to "be in community" with oneself? Tell a story about yourself or someone you have known that might illustrate the outer consequences of this inner harmony—or the lack of it.

8. Draw a line down the middle of a piece of paper. On the left-hand side, list the forces in your work situation that drive people toward community. On the right-hand side, list the forces that drive people away. What is the balance of forces? How might some of the positive forces be amplified? How might the negative forces be diminished?

9. Now do the same sort of analysis of the forces within yourself. On the left-hand side of the paper, list the inner forces that push you toward community. On the right-hand side, list the forces that push you away. What is the balance of forces? How might some of the positive forces be amplified? How might the negative forces be diminished?

10. What is your greatest fear about coming into community with others? What is your greatest hope? Which has the upper hand in your life at this moment—fear or hope? What might you do to deal with the fear and build on the hope?

D. *The hallmark of the "community of truth" is in its claim that reality is a web of communal relationships—and that we know reality only by being in community with it.*

11. In the course of your own education, what images did you receive—directly or indirectly—of how people gain knowledge? Draw visual representations of these images using simple graphics (see, for example, the diagrams on p. 103 and p. 105), and discuss what you see in each other's drawings.

12. Do you feel a "sense of community" with the subjects you teach and study? What is the nature of that relationship? How has your relationship with your subject enriched your life? Stretched your life? Challenged your life? Changed your life?

13. What are the benefits and drawbacks of having a personal relationship with the subject one teaches? Is it possible to know a subject well without a personal connection? If so, what are the benefits and drawbacks of that kind of knowledge?

E. *In the "community of truth," there are no pure objects of knowl-edge and no ultimate authorities. A subject, not an object, is the centerpoint of this community, and authority is vested in the process of the community itself.*

14. Do you think the "community of truth" is an accurate image of the way knowledge is gathered in your field? Why or why not?

15. Is there "objective knowledge" in the field you teach? If so, how is it achieved? Does the concept of the "community of truth" abandon or undermine the notion of objectivity, or does it redefine it? If the latter, how accurate is the redefinition, in your judgment?

16. As a student, did you have courses that made you a partici-pant in the "community of truth" gathered around that sub-ject? If so, describe how they worked. Compare their impact to courses that simply introduced you to the facts about the subject.

17. At what level of education—from preschool through gradu-ate school—are students most ready to be brought into the "community of truth"? Does the usefulness of this pedagogy depend on the developmental stage of one's students? At what level of education is this pedagogy most often employed?

F. *As the community of truth gathers around a "great thing," it is "the grace of great things" that evokes the virtues we cherish in education: celebrating diversity, embracing ambiguity, welcoming creative conflict, practicing honesty, and experiencing humility.*

18. If you find these virtues present in the place where you teach, how do you account for their presence?

19. If you find these virtues absent from the place where you teach, how do you account for their absence?

20. "We cannot know the great things of the universe until we know ourselves to be great things." Do you agree? Why or why not? If you agree, are teachers responsible for helping students develop this sense of self-worth in order to help them learn deeply and well?

G. *Teaching and learning are ultimately grounded in a sense of "the sacred" (pp. 113–116).*

21. Is "the sacred" a concept that has meaning in your experience? If so, tell a story about a personal experience of the sacred. What was that experience focused on? How did it make you feel? What were its consequences for your life and your work?

22. When was the last time you were taken by surprise by ideas or images or feelings? How does the culture you inhabit welcome or resist surprises? How might the concept of welcoming surprises change your way of teaching?

23. Reflect on the concept of "soft eyes" (p. 116). Think of a situation where having "soft eyes" might have helped you in the classroom. Describe what happened, how you reacted, and how you would have liked to react.

Chapter V

Teaching in Community
A Subject-Centered Education

A. *The best classroom is neither teacher-centered nor student-centered but subject-centered.*

1. Which of those three classroom types is most common in your experience? What do you perceive as the strengths and weaknesses of each? Think about the best classes you took as a student—how do they fit into this typology?

2. What do you see as the major obstacles to creating a subject-centered classroom? If you have tried to do so, how have you dealt with some of those obstacles? Where do you continue to feel blocked?

3. Do you agree that it is important to give the subject a "voice" in the classroom that is as real as the voices of teachers and students? If so, what ways have you found to let the subject "speak for itself" without constraining it to what you or the text has to say about it?

4. Are there ways in which technology can help put the subject at the center of the classroom and help connect teacher, students, and subject, or is technology antithetical to the "community of truth"?

B. *Every discipline has a "holographic logic" that allows us to see the shape of the whole by examining any significant piece of it. For that reason, we have the option of "teaching from the microcosm" as contrasted with "covering the field."*

5. Do you image your field as having this kind of holographic logic, or do you image it differently (for example, as an accumulation of information or a set of skills)? What implications does your way of imaging your field have for the way you teach?

6. Do you have an example of being taught "from the microcosm" when you were a student? What impact did this way of teaching have on you? What is your relation to that discipline today?

7. Reflect on a recent pedagogical moment in which "teaching less content at a deeper level" and "diving deep into particularity" seemed to work well for you—or where trying to teach this way might have yielded better results.

*C. By teaching from the microcosm, we can create classroom space
to demonstrate how our discipline is done—and to engage our
students in doing it—rather than just rehearsing the knowledge
of experts.*

8. Let someone in your group name a basic concept in his or
   her field that is usually taught by telling students about it.
   Brainstorm ways in which that concept might be taught
   through activities that teacher and students do together.

9. What forces within us and around us make it difficult to stop
   "covering the field" and turn instead to practicing the field
   with our students? What forces within us and around us
   might drive us to appreciate and embrace this approach?

10. What forces within and around our students drive them to
    resist this approach to teaching and learning? What forces
    within and around them might lead them to embrace this
    approach?

D. *If we are to persist in this mode of teaching—creating a space in which the community of truth is practiced—we need not only a rationale for what we are doing but also an awareness of the skillful means it requires.*

11. Think about a teacher who inspired you. What "skillful means," both obvious and subtle, did that teacher use to create an environment conducive to learning?

12. In small groups, ask each person to put forward a case study of a good moment in his or her teaching. Help that person identify the skillful means he or she used in that moment.

13. Review my (Parker Palmer's) analysis of the "skillful means" I called on during a good moment in my teaching—conceptualizing, listening, questioning, responding, reframing (pp. 135–138). As you reflect on a good moment in your own teaching, note in what ways your list is similar to or different from mine. What does this comparison reveal about your own identity and integrity as a teacher?

14. Identify one or two "skillful means" of your own that require a certain inner state to be used effectively. (For example, the skill of not answering a student's question immediately, in hopes of creating a larger dialogue, requires "letting go" inwardly of the need to control.) Are there inner issues you need to work on to sharpen the use of your skillful means?

E. In order to move closer to the community of truth in the class-room, we must make ourselves as dependent on our students as they are on us.

15. Discuss the limits and potentials of being "in community" with your students. To what degree is this possible? Desirable? An actuality in your teaching life?

16. Have you found ways to use grades creatively to emphasize learning rather than judging, collaborating rather than competing? Do you agree that grades make students more dependent on us than we are on them?

17. In what ways do your students depend on you? Try to go beyond conventional professional answers (for example, "They depend on me to be well prepared in my field and dispassionate in grading"), and reach instead into the realm of personal meaning (for example, "They depend on me to encourage them and affirm their lives")—if you believe such to be true.

18. In what ways do you depend on your students? Try to go beyond conventional professional answers (for example, "I depend on them to be on time and to have their homework done"), and reach instead into the realm of personal meaning (for example, "I depend on them to keep me connected with the younger generation")—if you believe such to be true.

 SEGMENT 15: THE HARDEST PART OF TEACHING

- Are teachers and schools in your community pressed to deliver high student scores on standardized tests? Have you personally experienced any of the consequences of high-stakes testing?
- What do you see as the consequences of judging teachers and schools by these tests? Has it involved "a trivialization of the work and the crushing of the lives of kids" in your school setting? Or have some of the consequences been more positive than that?
- How can teachers find the courage to do more than "teach to the test" when their jobs may depend on test outcomes? How can they make space to teach young people "to know what they need to know to be full human beings in a very difficult world"?

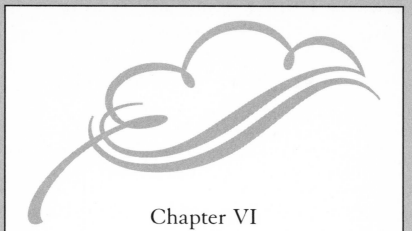

Chapter VI

Learning in Community
The Conversation of Colleagues

A. *Teaching is a highly "privatized" profession. We teach our classes out of sight of our colleagues and rarely discuss teaching with them.*

1. How often do you visit a colleague's classes, or vice versa? Has your teaching ever been evaluated by a colleague, or vice versa? How often do you sit with colleagues to explore teaching, and at what depth? How do you feel about the picture that emerges as you respond to these questions?

2. If teaching is privatized at your institution, what are some of the sources of this situation, and what are its consequences for teachers and teaching? If not, what factors have made your institution different?

3. Are there advantages to the privatization of teaching—real or perceived? What price do we pay for it? Are there forces at work, either within us or around us, that may diminish privatization and create a more collegial community?

B. Three elements are essential if we are to create a collegial community of discourse about teaching. The first is topics of conversation that take us beyond technique.

4. Critical Moments in Teaching and Learning, Part I: Draw a long horizontal line on a chalkboard to represent the movement of a course from start to finish. Ask the group to brainstorm the critical moments in that journey of teaching and learning while you locate each moment with a mark on the line, identifying it with a word or a brief phrase. A "critical moment" is one in which a learning opportunity for students will either open up or shut down, depending in part on how the teacher handles it. After brainstorming, explore the dynamics of a course as they are imaged on the chalkboard, noting such aspects as their complexity, their degree of predictability, and their vulnerability to outside forces (see pp. 150–152).

5. Critical Moments in Teaching and Learning, Part II: Examine the timeline, creating and naming clusters of critical moments (for example, "starting a course," "dealing with conflict," or "the fallout from evaluation"). Invite people to form small groups around a cluster of interest to them. In these groups, each person gets a chance to explore aloud what he or she has done, for better or worse, in response to the issues in question, while others listen. Participants are free to report on their own classroom experiences, and to ask other people honest, open questions about *their* reports. But they are *not* free to criticize what other people did or advise them on what they "should have done." The goal is not "fixing" but listening and "hearing people into speech," to help everyone become more reflective about his or her practice.

6. Metaphors of Good Teaching, Part I: Think of a moment when you were teaching at your best. Then fill in the blank: "When I am teaching at my best, I am like a _____." Don't censor your metaphor, even if it seems nonsensical. In small groups, help each person tease out the implications of

her or her metaphor, noting what it reveals about that person's gifts and limits as a teacher.

7. Metaphors of Good Teaching, Part II: In small groups, give each person a chance to tell about a negative teaching experience. Following each story, explore the following question: "In this instance, what would a [insert the storyteller's metaphor here] have done?" Stay close to the metaphor, and avoid talking about technique. For example, with a metaphor like "sheepdog," stay with—and play with!—answers like "barking" and "nipping at their heels" rather than translating these images into actual teaching behaviors. Allow the power of metaphor to loose the imagination, and have some fun!

C. The second element essential to creating a community of discourse about teaching is ground rules for conversation, rules that keep us from defeating ourselves before the conversation has a chance to go deep.

8. How would you characterize the quantity and quality of conversation between colleagues at your institution? Can you name some of the tacit "ground rules" of that conversation? Which of those ground rules are worth keeping? Which would you like to get rid of?

9. If you find the overall collegial conversation unsatisfactory, are there pockets within your institution where good conversation flourishes? If so, what makes those places or occasions different?

10. Discuss the ground rules your study group has been using to respect each other's voices and vulnerabilities. Which of these rules have worked, and which have not? Have any of them affected the way you interact with students, with colleagues, or with other people in your life? Can any of them be exported to your institution?

SEGMENT 16: THE GROUND RULES
FOR COMMUNITY

- Think about questions you have asked and been asked in conversations with colleagues, both formal and informal. How do they compare with the norm of "honest, open questions"? Did they facilitate candid and fruitful exchanges? If not, what might happen to change this dimension of your collegial community and make it more life-giving?
- In the video, the soul is compared to a wild animal, calling it very resilient but very shy. Can you imagine creating a setting in which the shy creature called personal identity and integrity will feel safe enough to show up? How can we create such settings for ourselves, our students, and our colleagues?

D. *The third element essential to creating a community of discourse about teaching is leaders who expect and invite others to join the conversation. Leaders need to discern the difference between what teachers say about themselves and what their real needs are and then provide excuses and permissions for real needs to be met.*

11. Have you known a leader, in or out of education, who invites others into community as part of getting a job done or pursuing a mission? In what particular ways did he or she extend the invitation to community? What personal qualities made that style of leadership possible for that person?

12. At your educational institution, who are the leaders, both formal and informal, who have an opportunity to help create a community of discourse about teaching? Do you include yourself on either of those lists? Why or why not?

13. What "permissions and excuses" have leaders at your institution offered to promote good talk about good teaching? What "permissions and excuses" might you, or your study group, offer to bring other colleagues into this conversation?

THE COURAGE TO TEACH GUIDE FOR REFLECTION AND RENEWAL

E. The Courage to Teach *describes several kinds of institutional arrangements that promote "good talk about good teaching"— workshops, teaching and learning centers, faculty consultants, and so on—as well as several approaches to the evaluation of teaching (pp. 163–166).*

14. What programs does your institution have to help teachers grow in their work? What sort of "fit" is there between these programs, their number and nature, and what the institution says about the value it attaches to teaching? How do your colleagues feel about what goes on in these programs? How do you feel?

15. Have you heard or read about other kinds of teacher development programs? If so, discuss their benefits and drawbacks as you see them. Which of these programs might work at your institution? Which would not? Why?

16. What approach does your institution take to the evaluation of teaching? What are the strengths and weaknesses of this approach? In particular, does this approach embrace the varieties of good teaching? Does it help teachers grow in their work? Does it contribute to a community of discourse about teaching, or does it contribute to the privatization and isolation of the teacher's work?

17. How are students involved in the evaluation of teachers at your institution? Is their involvement useful? Why or why not? If it is not, can you think of creative ways to bring students in on this process?

SEGMENT 17: ENCOURAGING SELF-REFLECTION

- Reflect on the following paraphrase of remarks made by Thomas Merton: "We're called to give our hearts to the world, but first we have to have our hearts in our own possession. We cannot give to others what we ourselves don't possess." In your experience, does professional life tend to rob us of our own hearts? If so, how might we reclaim them?

- As you read the first stanza of May Sarton's poem "Now I Become Myself," what arises for you about your own life journey, about where you have been and where you are now?

Now I become myself. It's taken
Time, many years and places;
I have been dissolved and shaken,
Worn other people's faces. . . .

Chapter VII

Divided No More
Teaching from a Heart of Hope

A. *If we want to reform education in the face of great obstacles, we need to develop a "movement mentality," a way of experiencing resistance not as a source of defeat but as a source of energy.*

1. The "heart mantra" in *The Courage to Teach* names four phases in a teacher's life: teaching from the heart, losing heart, seeking to take heart, and giving heart to students. Identify and explore the phase or phases that characterize your vocation at this moment.

2. Despair comes when we "internalize the logic of the organization" and then find our vision of hope blocked by the same organization. Give examples of what it means for a person to "internalize the logic" of an organization. What are the personal trade-offs involved in doing so?

3. Movements and their founders "abandon the logic of organizations so that they can gather the momentum necessary to alter the logic of organizations." Is it possible to free yourself from "organizational logic" while still remaining a part of the organization? What would it mean to do so?

4. Do you have examples of times in your own life, in or out of formal education, when resistance to something you wanted led you not to abandon your goal but to redouble your efforts? What helped this happen?

 SEGMENT 18: TURNOVER AMONG TEACHERS

- What do you believe accounts for the high turnover among K–12 teachers, with 50 percent of them leaving the profession within the first five years?
- What kind of support do teachers need to stay in education? What would it mean to tend teachers "the way a gardener tends plants"? How can we support the teacher's heart?

THE COURAGE TO TEACH GUIDE FOR REFLECTION AND RENEWAL

B. *Review the four stages of a movement, as summarized on pages 172–173 of* The Courage to Teach. *Before examining them one by one, reflect on the general shape of social movements.*

5. Think of a movement you have participated in or one about which you are knowledgeable. Do you see any of these four stages in the evolution of that movement? What can you learn from that movement about a movement for educational reform?

6. Is there a movement for reform—or a limited version of one—going on in your sector of the educational world or at your institution? If not, why not? If so, at what stage is this movement? What will it take to move it to the next stage?

C. *The first stage of a movement involves a deeply personal decision to live "divided no more."*

7. Think of someone you know personally—or a historical figure whose story you know—who decided to live "divided no more." What led this person to that decision, with the risks it entails? What was the source of his or her courage?

8. Can you identify a moment when you decided to live "divided no more"? What were the circumstances that brought you to that moment? What resources and supports helped you in that moment? What changes, internal and external, resulted from your decision? How lasting were those changes?

9. Is there an area of your life today where you feel a need to live divided no more? What resources and supports do you need to help you examine and act on that need?

SEGMENT 19: LIVING "DIVIDED NO MORE"

- The Rosa Parks story is used to illustrate what it means to live "divided no more"—with the moment when she stayed in her chosen seat on the bus representing her decision to "no longer behave on the outside in a way that contradicted the truth she knew about herself on the inside." Reflect on this story and its meaning for you.
- Have there been parallel moments in your life, moments when you needed to decided whether or not to "collaborate in your own diminishment"? What decisions have you made in such moments? How do you feel about them now?
- Are you currently in a situation where you need to decide once again whether or not you will live a divided life? What would help you make that decision in a way that gives you life?

D. The second stage of a movement involves forming "communities of congruence."

10. Do you feel the need for such a community to sustain your own vocation? If so, how might you find or create such a community? What are the impediments to doing so? If you already have a community of congruence, what helped you find or create it? What role does it play in your life?

11. Are there structures at your institution, or outside of it, that could shelter communities of congruence for teachers who make the decision to live divided no more (see p. 178)? What structures seem most promising in this regard, and how might they be more fully used for this purpose?

12. Your study group may be functioning as a community of congruence for you. If so, what impact has it had on your own decision to live "divided no more"? What impact has it had on your own process of "going public" with your commitment to educational reform?

**SEGMENT 20: THE INNER JOURNEY
IN COMMUNITY**

- The phrase "an inner journey" usually suggests solitude. Why is it important, perhaps even necessary, to have a community to support your inner journey? Or is it?
- Do you have such a community in your life—a community that can help you hear your own truth, distinguish between truth and illusion, and support you in your own commitments?
- If you do not have such a community, can you imagine ways of finding one or creating one? What might you gain by doing so? What might you have to give up?

E. The third stage of a movement involves "going public" with our values and commitments.

13. Have you ever been influenced by someone who has gone public with his or her core values? What was that experience like? What impact did it have on your own thought and action?

14. Have you ever gone public with your own core values? What was that experience like? What impact did it have on the people or situation around you?

15. Educators have often failed to make common cause with individuals and institutions outside of education (for example, in the business world) who might be allies in a movement for good teaching (pp. 183–186). Do you agree with this claim? If so, why do you think this is, and what do you think can and should be done about it? If not, what is the evidence that "common cause" is being made, and what are its benefits and liabilities for education?

16. Going public is vital to a healthy movement because it allows the movement to be critiqued and corrected by the larger community. Is this happening in the movement for educational reform—or does it need to happen? What specific corrections do you think this movement needs?

F. The fourth stage of a movement involves the emergence of a system of "alternative rewards."

17. As you reflect on your own vocation as a teacher, what have been the most meaningful rewards you have received, rewards that have helped keep you engaged with this work?

18. What are people rewarded for at the institution where you teach, and how are they rewarded? Does your institution reward people for good teaching? If so, how does it do so?

19. If you regard yourself as involved in a movement for educational reform, at any level, what rewards do you receive from that involvement? How important are they to you?

So we come full circle, to the place where this book began: to the power within each of us that, in communion with powers beyond ourselves, co-creates the world—for better or worse. The poet Rumi says, "If you are here unfaithfully with us, / you're causing terrible damage."

The evidence of his claim is all around us, not least in education: when we are unfaithful to the inward teacher and to the community of truth, we do lamentable damage to ourselves, to our students, and to the great things of the world that our knowledge holds in trust.

But Rumi would surely agree that the converse is equally true. If you are here faithfully with us, you are bringing abundant blessing. It is a blessing known to generations of students whose lives have been transformed by people who had the courage to teach—the courage to teach from the most truthful places in the landscape of self and world, the courage to invite students to discover, explore, and inhabit those places in the living of their own lives.

 SEGMENT 21: KEEPING YOUR INNER FLAME ALIVE

"Will I conspire in my own diminishment by succumbing to external forces—or will I find ways to go on an inner journey, rekindling my inner light and gathering a community around me that can help keep my flame alive?"

- Is this a critical question for you at this moment in your life?
- If so, where are you in relation to that question right now, and what would help you keep living into it?
- If not, what is the question you need to be asking yourself right now, and what would help you keep probing it?

Afterword to the
Tenth Anniversary Edition

The New Professional

Education for Transformation

A. *A significant sign that a movement is under way is the growing body of research and literature devoted to integrative teaching and learning, offering evidence that the national discourse on education is expanding to include inner-life issues.*

　　1. As you think about the books you've read and the courses or workshops you've attended in recent years, have you noticed a growing acknowledgment of the importance of inner-life issues in your profession?

　　2. What have you gained from doing such reading or participating in such workshops?

　　3. What are your concerns or criticisms about this movement as you experience it?

B. *The degree of "relational trust" among the people who work at a school is one of the key factors in whether or not that school serves its students well.*

4. What experience do you have in settings marked by relational trust—or the absence of it? How did that experience affect your feelings about yourself, your students, your colleagues? How did it affect the quality of the work you and others did there?

5. What does it take to create relational trust in a setting where it is in short supply? What does it take to maintain relational trust in a setting where it is well established? What kind of outer work is required? What kind of inner work is required?

6. In settings where external factors—such as No Child Left Behind—threaten relational trust, are there ways to maintain a generous and open collegial community? In such settings, is it still possible to open up the trustworthy spaces where your students can learn and grow?

C. *The most compelling evidence of a social change movement comes when leaders—positional or not, on the inside or the outside—start working for the transformation of particular institutional policies and practices.*

7. Are there people you know and admire who hold or have held positions of institutional influence, who used that power to effect positive institutional change? Tell a story about such a person, with special attention to his or her inner qualities.

8. Are there people you know and admire who had little or no conventional power but who still managed to change the institutions and societies in which they lived and worked? Tell a story about such a person, with special attention to his or her inner qualities.

9. How do you assess your own capacity to be such a leader, positional or otherwise, on the inside or the outside? What powers do you possess—or might you claim—to work toward positive institutional change?

D. *The Afterword to the tenth anniversary edition of* The Courage to Teach *attempts to go beyond the "generalities of the movement model" toward a more focused agenda for change called "the education of a new professional."*

10. Using your own language and your own imagery and drawing on your own experience, how would you describe the "new professional"?

11. Do you think such people are needed? Do you think it is possible for professionals of this sort to survive and even thrive in our institutions as they are?

12. Think back to your own professional education. Were parts of it supportive of the idea of a new professional? Were parts of it toxic to that notion?

E. *The rationale for educating a new professional is illustrated here by a case study of a tragic failure in health care—and arguably, in medical education—failures that have parallels in every profession and every form of professional education.*

13. As you read the case study, what is your response to the resident? Do you regard her as the victim of the system that pushed her too far and too fast and failed to support her? Or do you hold her partly responsible for the patient's death?

14. What is the right way to assess and assign responsibility for a failure of this sort—not out of a need to cast blame but in order to help us understand what's needed in our education system to prepare professionals to confront such situations?

15. Have you had experiences as an educator where, in the broadest sense, a student's "life was in the balance" and you lacked the preparation or support to hold that responsibility well? What kind of preparation or situational support would have been most helpful to you?

16. How can you create learning situations in the classroom and other venues that might challenge and prepare your students to think and act independently, to be moral agents who do not feel "owned and operated" by the institutions in which they will work?

F. The Afterword contains five "immodest proposals" for the educa-
tion of a new professional. The first involves helping our students
"uncover, examine, and debunk the myth that institutions are
external to us and constrain us, as if they possessed autonomous
powers that render us helpless."

17. Many of us think of institutions as external forces that are
    over us and against us. Do you agree with the assertion that
    "institutions are us"? As you think about your school, the
    educational system, or even politics at large, do you see ways
    in which these institutions reflect our individual and collec-
    tive shadows?

18. More specifically, think of one or two qualities in your col-
    leagues or your work environment that you find particularly
    difficult (for example, contentiousness or secrecy or distrust).
    Can you imagine ways in which you might be unconsciously
    exacerbating those problems? If so, how might you bring
    this more fully to consciousness and do something about it?

19. How might you introduce your students to this concept in a
    way that would help them work on their own "projections"?
    For example, can you imagine examining with them the
    ways in which your and their projections create the dynam-
    ics of that classroom, for better and for worse?

G. *The second immodest proposal: "If we are to educate a new professional, we must take our students' emotional intelligence as seriously as we take their cognitive intelligence."*

20. If we are to help our students develop emotional intelligence, we need to be emotionally literate ourselves. We need to be aware of our own emotions, take responsibility for them, and understand how they affect our attitudes and interactions with others. How would you assess yourself in this regard, especially when it comes to dealing with your own emotions in the classroom?

21. As you look back on your own journey and some of the important formal and informal learning you have done along the way, can you identify moments when your own emotional intelligence was the key to what you learned? What does this exercise tell you about the nature and depth of your emotional intelligence?

22. Think back on your own education, identifying times when the classrooms you sat in were either hospitable or hostile to the emotions. What made the difference—in the environment, in the teacher, in the students? How did you know what would be allowed and supported emotionally? What were the clues?

23. Fear can be a pervasive emotion in a school or work setting, paralyzing the mind, blocking learning, and creating corrosive doubt about one's competence to do the work. How do you or might you alleviate fear in your classroom, creating a safe learning community in which students can explore their "feelings about themselves, the work they do, the people with whom they work, the institutional settings in which they work, and the world in which they live"?

THE COURAGE TO TEACH GUIDE FOR REFLECTION AND RENEWAL

H. *The third immodest proposal is that "we start taking seriously the intelligence in emotional intelligence."*

24. It is not enough that students learn to name and claim their emotions. They must develop the skill of "mining" their emotions for knowledge. Can you think of a significant example in your own life when paying attention to your emotions helped you gain important cognitive knowledge about external reality?

25. Ask your students to study the biography of someone who has made a positive difference in the world. Ask them to identify the kinds of intelligence that made this person effective. Did emotional intelligence play a role? If so, how and why?

I. The fourth immodest proposal: We must "offer our students the knowledge, skills, and sensibilities required to cultivate communities of discernment."

26. A community of discernment can help us "distinguish fool's gold from the real thing." Do you have such a community? If so, how does that community work? What are the principles and practices that make a community of discernment possible?

27. As you think about a community of discernment that has been part of your life, do you get any clues about establishing a similar network of relationships in your classroom?

28. If you are unable either to name a community of discernment in your own life or to imagine how one might emerge in your classroom, how do you understand this void in a profession—education—that is supposed to be rooted in a community of knowing, teaching, and learning that helps its members distinguish reality from illusion and truth from falsehood?

J. *The fifth immodest proposal: "We must help our students under-stand what it means to live and work with the question of an undivided life always before them."*

29. "Our students need to see how we, their elders, deal with [the] vagaries of fate while refusing to sell out either our professions or our own identity and integrity. And they need to see how, when we fail and fall down, as everyone does, we manage to get up again." What are some ways that you do or might make your life experience in this regard available to your students?

30. What opportunities do students have at your institution and in your classroom to offer constructive criticism and be taken seriously as agents of change within the setting where they are now "on the job" as students? Can you imagine institutionalizing a meaningful process of this sort?

Appendixes

Appendix A

Suggestions for Organizing a Courage to Teach *Book Discussion Group*

David Leo-Nyquist

D avid Leo-Nyquist is a Courage & Renewal facilitator who does professional development work with teachers and school leaders in Vermont. In a former role as a teacher-educator, he organized a series of *Courage to Teach* book discussions on his campus. The following are his helpful suggestions on how to develop such a process in your work setting.

- As organizer of a study group, tell yourself what you tell your students: read the book carefully, marking passages and making marginal annotations as you read so you can refer to them later. Then, just like your students, do exactly that!

- Read through Parts One and Two of this *Guide*. Part One has helpful suggestions for how to create and hold the space for your discussion group. Part Two has helpful questions and activities for each chapter and includes references to and questions for the video segments in the accompanying DVD. The questions apply to both the book and the DVD, so the discussion of one can build on the other. You may find it helpful to use segments of the DVD to spice up your discussions.

- Find one or two other colleagues who might be interested in reading the book in advance and in sharing responsibility with you as a small-group leader. You can do it alone, but two or three planning together is best.

- Plan out a schedule for meetings based on your sense of what will work in your school, organization, or community. We met monthly on the same weekday for four two-hour after-school discussions from 4:00 to 6:00 P.M. I think that ninety-minute sessions would also work, but it's hard for me to imagine doing the book justice with shorter meetings than that. We read the entire book in four "chunks" (usually two chapters a month), but the chapters are rich enough to devote a month to each chapter. The book has seven chapters and a substantial Afterword, so decide in advance how you want to divide them for assigned reading.

- Distribute a written invitation to your colleagues about what you have in mind (see the sample letter in this Appendix). Include all the information they'll need in order to make a decision about participating, including times, dates, format, and purpose. Consider attaching a short excerpt from the book (not more than a page or two, something that can be read in five minutes or so) or give them a copy of the article "The Heart of a Teacher: Identity and Integrity in Teaching," reprinted in Appendix B.
- Ask your colleagues to commit to participating well in advance of the first meeting. Consider buying enough copies of the book for everyone, to save the trouble of ordering individually. Encourage everyone to have a copy: sharing copies is complicated, and the book is definitely a "keeper."
- You might be able to share the book cost with participants through school support, especially if your principal or other administrators are participating. Some booksellers give discounts for bulk orders.
- When you deliver the books (preferably at least a week before the first meeting), give participants a set of written questions to guide their reading (you can take these from Part Two of this *Guide*), and ask them to think about these questions and any others that might occur to them before they come to the first meeting.
- Although each discussion will move in its own direction based on the needs and interests of the participants, it is useful to have questions to get started and to give a direction when needed. Part Two of this *Guide* has questions for both the book and the corresponding DVD segments. These video segments can be used to help get the conversation rolling.
- If more than ten people attend, you may decide to break into smaller groups. We usually met for about fifteen minutes as a large group of twenty-five to thirty and then split into

smaller groups of five to eight for at least an hour. We reconvened at the end for a whole-group sharing and closure.

- Consider planning in advance some key issues related to the assigned reading that you would like to raise verbally with the large group that may help jump-start the small-group discussions.

- Begin and end your meetings on time, and have some good food and drink available. Treat your participants well, and they'll look forward to coming back.

Sample Invitation Letter for a
Courage to Teach Book Discussion Group

Dear Colleagues:

As we all begin yet one more academic year in our teaching careers, we would like to invite you to participate in a dialogue with your peers that we believe you will find both useful and inspirational. We believe that a thoughtful teacher dialogue has the potential to strengthen our teaching lives, and we wish to create a public forum that nurtures and sustains rich professional conversations about our shared commitment to a life of teaching.

To that end, we have a simple proposal for you. This fall, we are initiating four monthly "teacher dialogues" that will bring together teachers to focus conversationally on our shared passion for teaching. The events are sponsored by _____ .

The meetings will take place on _____ in the _____ . The format will be small-group facilitated discussions centered on an assigned reading from a common text.

The book we have selected is the tenth anniversary edition of Parker J. Palmer's renowned book *The Courage to Teach: Exploring the Inner Landscape of a Teacher's Life*. We have long been impressed by the rich possibilities this text provides to support just the kinds of conversations we have in mind.

We are enclosing an article by Parker J. Palmer, "The Heart of a Teacher: Identity and Integrity in Teaching" (which is drawn from *The Courage to Teach* and appeared in *Change* magazine) to give you a taste for the range of issues we will be discussing.

One of our sponsoring organizations, _____ , will cover much of the book cost (your share will be $___). You will receive the book from us prior to our first meeting.

Refreshments will be provided, and we will finish our conversations promptly at _____. The commitment we are asking from you is to "sign on" for discussions to be held on the following dates: _____.

We hope that you will give serious consideration to our invitation and that if you're both interested and free for the proposed meeting dates, you will contact us *as soon as possible* with a confirmation of that interest. Because we want to keep the total group size to fewer than forty participants, we will handle the responses on a first come, first served basis. We ask that you sign up only if you're able to come to all four discussions.

To confirm your participation, please contact _____.

We look forward to joining you in conversation on this important book.

Sincerely,

SAMPLE FOLLOW-UP LETTER FOR A
COURAGE TO TEACH BOOK DISCUSSION GROUP

Dear Colleagues:

Thank you for responding to our invitation to participate in the "Teacher Dialogue Series," centered on Parker J. Palmer's book *The Courage to Teach.*

The first meeting of the series will be held on _____ in the _____.

To prepare for this discussion, we ask that you read Chapter I of the text. Enclosed are some questions to help guide you in your preparation. We may not be able to discuss all the questions; please note those that are of particular interest to you.

Your copy of *The Courage to Teach* accompanies this letter. Your share of the cost of this book is $___, which can be paid in cash or by check at the first gathering.

Subsequent meetings will be held on _____. All will be in the _____.

If you have any questions, please feel free to contact me at _____ or via e-mail at _____.

We look forward to seeing you on _____.

Sincerely,

_____

Note: We suggest you enclose a copy of the questions for Chapter I, item A, on page 26 of this *Guide.*

Appendix B

The Heart of a Teacher
Identity and Integrity in Teaching

This article originally appeared in the Nov.-Dec. 1997 issue of *Change* magazine as a summary of *The Courage to Teach* at the time of the book's publication. We suggest that you include a copy of this article, or excerpts from it, with the invitation to your *Courage to Teach* discussion group. It will help participants get a sense both of the book and of the direction the group discussion might take.

We Teach Who We Are

I am a teacher at heart, and there are moments in the classroom when I can hardly hold the joy. When my students and I discover uncharted territory to explore, when the pathway out of a thicket opens up before us, when our experience is illumined by the lightning-life of the mind—then teaching is the finest work I know.

But at other moments, the classroom is so lifeless or painful or confused—and I am so powerless to do anything about it—that my claim to be a teacher seems a transparent sham. Then the enemy is everywhere: in those students from some alien planet, in that subject I thought I knew, and in the personal pathology that keeps me earning my living this way. What a fool I was to imagine that I had mastered this occult art—harder to divine than tea leaves and impossible for mortals to do even passably well!

The tangles of teaching have three important sources. The first two are commonplace, but the third, and most fundamental, is rarely given its due. First, the subjects we teach are as large and complex as life, so our knowledge of them is always flawed and partial. No matter how we devote ourselves to reading and research, teaching requires a command of content that always eludes our grasp. Second, the students we teach are larger than life and even more complex. To see them clearly and see them whole, and respond to them wisely in the moment, requires a fusion of Freud and Solomon that few of us achieve.

If students and subjects accounted for all the complexities of teaching, our standard ways of coping would do—keep up with our fields as best we can, and learn enough techniques to stay ahead of the student psyche. But there is another reason for these complexities: we teach who we are.

Teaching, like any truly human activity, emerges from one's inwardness, for better or worse. As I teach, I project the condition of my soul onto my students, my subject, and our way of being together. The entanglements I experience in the classroom are often no more or less than the convolutions of my inner life. Viewed from this angle, teaching holds a mirror to the soul. If I am willing to look in

Appendix B

that mirror, and not run from what I see, I have a chance to gain self-knowledge—and knowing myself is as crucial to good teaching as knowing my students and my subject.

In fact, knowing my students and my subject depends heavily on self-knowledge. When I do not know myself, I cannot know who my students are. I will see them through a glass darkly, in the shadows of my unexamined life—and when I cannot see them clearly I cannot teach them well. When I do not know myself, I cannot know my subject—not at the deepest levels of embodied, personal meaning. I will know it only abstractly, from a distance, a congeries of concepts as far removed from the world as I am from personal truth.

We need to open a new frontier in our exploration of good teaching: the inner landscape of a teacher's life. To chart that landscape fully, three important paths must be taken—intellectual, emotional, and spiritual—and none can be ignored. Reduce teaching to intellect and it becomes a cold abstraction; reduce it to emotions and it becomes narcissistic; reduce it to the spiritual and it loses its anchor to the world. Intellect, emotion, and spirit depend on each other for wholeness. They are interwoven in the human self and in education at its best, and we need to interweave them in our pedagogical discourse as well.

By *intellectual* I mean the way we think about teaching and learning—the form and content of our concepts of how people know and learn, of the nature of our students and our subjects. By *emotional* I mean the way we and our students feel as we teach and learn—feelings that can either enlarge or diminish the exchange between us. By *spiritual* I mean the diverse ways we answer the heart's longing to be connected with the largeness of life—a longing that animates love and work, especially the work called teaching.

TEACHING BEYOND TECHNIQUE

After three decades of trying to learn my craft, every class comes down to this: my students and I, face to face, engaged in an ancient and exacting exchange called education. The techniques I have mastered do not disappear, but neither do they suffice. Face to face with my students, only one resource is at my immediate command: my identity, my selfhood, my sense of this "I" who teaches—without which I have no sense of the "Thou" who learns.

Here is a secret hidden in plain sight: *good teaching cannot be reduced to technique; good teaching comes from the identity and integrity of the teacher.* In every class I teach, my ability to connect with my students, and to connect them with the subject, depends less on the methods I use than on the degree to which I know and trust my selfhood—and am willing to make it available and vulnerable in the service of learning.

My evidence for this claim comes, in part, from years of asking students to tell me about their good teachers. Listening to those stories, it becomes impossible to claim that all good teachers use similar techniques: some lecture non-stop and others speak very little, some stay close to their material and others loose the imagination, some teach with the carrot and others with the stick.

But in every story I have heard, good teachers share one trait: a strong sense of personal identity infuses their work. "Dr. A is really *there* when she teaches," a student tells me, or "Mr. B has such enthusiasm for his subject," or "You can tell that this is really Prof. C's life."

One student I heard about said she could not describe her good teachers because they were so different from each other. But she could describe her bad teachers because they were all the same: "Their words float somewhere in front of their faces, like the balloon speech in cartoons." With one remarkable image she said it all. Bad teachers distance themselves from the subject they are teaching—and, in the process, from their students.

Good teachers join self, subject, and students in the fabric of life because they teach from an integral and undivided self; they manifest in their own lives, and evoke in their students, a "capacity for connectedness." They are able to weave a complex web of connections between themselves, their subjects, and their students, so that students can learn to weave a world for themselves. The methods used by these weavers vary widely: lectures, Socratic dialogues, laboratory experiments, collaborative problem-solving, creative chaos. The connections made by good teachers are held not in their methods but in their hearts—meaning heart in its ancient sense, the place where intellect and emotion and spirit and will converge in the human self.

If good teaching cannot be reduced to technique, I no longer need suffer the pain of having my peculiar gift as a teacher crammed into the Procrustean bed of someone else's method and the standards prescribed by it. That pain is felt throughout education today as we insist upon the method *du jour*—leaving people who teach differently feeling devalued, forcing them to measure up to norms not their own.

I will never forget one professor who, moments before I was to start a workshop on teaching, unloaded years of pent-up workshop animus on me: "I am an organic chemist. Are you going to spend the next two days telling me that I am supposed to teach organic chemistry through role-playing?" His wry question was not only related to his distinctive discipline but also to his distinctive self: we must find an approach to teaching that respects the diversity of teachers as well as disciplines, which methodological reductionism fails to do.

The capacity for connectedness manifests itself in diverse and wondrous ways—as many ways as there are forms of personal identity. Two great teachers stand out from my own undergraduate experience. They differed radically from each other in technique, but both were gifted at connecting students, teacher, and subject in a community of learning.

One of those teachers assigned a lot of reading in her course on methods of social research and, when we gathered around the seminar table on the first day, said, "Any comments or questions?" She had the courage to wait out our stupefied (and stupefying) silence, minute after minute after minute, gazing around the table with a benign look on her face—and then, after the passage of a small eternity, to rise, pick up her books, and say, as she walked toward the door, "Class dismissed."

This scenario more or less repeated itself a second time, but by the third time we met, our high SAT scores had kicked in, and we realized that the big dollars we were paying for this education would be wasted if we did not get with the program. So we started doing the reading, making comments, asking questions—and our teacher proved herself to be a brilliant interlocutor, co-researcher, and guide in the midst of confusions, a "weaver" of connectedness in her own interactive and inimitable way.

My other great mentor taught the history of social thought. He did not know the meaning of silence and he was awkward at interaction; he lectured incessantly while we sat in rows and took notes. Indeed, he became so engaged with his material that he was often impatient with our questions. But his classes were nonetheless permeated with a sense of connectedness and community.

How did he manage this alchemy? Partly by giving lectures that went far beyond presenting the data of social theory into staging the drama of social thought. He told stories from the lives of great thinkers as well as explaining their ideas; we could almost see Karl Marx, sitting alone in the British Museum Library, writing *Das Kapital*. Through active imagination we were brought into community with the thinker himself, and with the personal and social conditions that stimulated his thought.

But the drama of my mentor's lectures went farther still. He would make a strong Marxist statement, and we would transcribe it in our notebooks as if it were holy writ. Then a puzzled look would pass over his face. He would pause, step to one side, turn and look back at the space he had just exited—and argue with his own statement from an Hegelian point of view! This was not an artificial device but a genuine expression of the intellectual drama that continually occupied this teacher's mind and heart.

"Drama" does not mean histrionics, of course, and remembering that fact can help us name a form of connectedness that is palpable and powerful without being overtly interactive, or even face-to-face. When I go to the theater, I sometimes feel strongly connected to the action, as if my own life were being portrayed on stage. But I have no desire to raise my hand and respond to the line just spoken, or run up the aisle, jump onto the stage, and join in the action. Sitting in the audience, I am already on stage "in person," connected in an inward and invisible way that we rarely credit as the powerful form of community that it is. With a good drama, I do not need overt interaction to be "in community" with those characters and their lives.

I used to wonder how my mentor, who was so awkward in his face-to-face relations with students, managed to simulate community so well. Now I understand: he was in community without us! Who needs twenty-year-olds from the suburbs when you are hang-

APPENDIX B

ing out constantly with the likes of Marx and Hegel, Durkheim, Weber and Troeltsch? This is "community" of the highest sort—this capacity for connectedness that allows one to converse with the dead, to speak and listen in an invisible network of relationships that enlarges one's world and enriches one's life. (We should praise, not deride, First Ladies who "talk" with Eleanor Roosevelt; the ability to learn from wise but long-gone souls is nothing less than a classic mark of a liberal education!)

Yet my great professor, though he communed more intimately with the great figures of social thought than with the people close at hand, cared deeply about his students. The passion with which he lectured was not only for his subject, but for us to know his subject. He wanted us to meet and learn from the constant companions of his intellect and imagination, and he made those introductions in a way that was deeply integral to his own nature. He brought us into a form of community that did not require small numbers of students sitting in a circle and learning through dialogue.

These two great teachers were polar opposites in substance and in style. But both created the connectedness, the community, that is essential to teaching and learning. They did so by trusting and teaching from true self, from the identity and integrity that is the source of all good work—and by employing quite different techniques that allowed them to reveal rather than conceal who they were.

Their genius as teachers, and their profound gifts to me, would have been diminished and destroyed had their practice been forced into the Procrustean bed of the method of the moment. The proper place for technique is not to subdue subjectivity, not to mask and distance the self from the work, but—as one grows in self-knowledge—to help bring forth and amplify the gifts of self on which good work depends.

TEACHING AND TRUE SELF

The claim that good teaching comes from the identity and integrity of the teacher might sound like a truism, and a pious one at that: good teaching comes from good people. But by "identity" and "integrity" I do not mean only our noble features, or the good deeds we do, or the brave faces we wear to conceal our confusions and complexities. Identity and integrity have as much to do with our shadows and limits, our wounds and fears, as with our strengths and potentials.

By *identity* I mean an evolving nexus where all the forces that constitute my life converge in the mystery of self: my genetic makeup, the nature of the man and woman who gave me life, the culture in which I was raised, people who have sustained me and people who have done me harm, the good and ill I have done to others, and to myself, the experience of love and suffering—and much, much more. In the midst of that complex field, identity is a moving intersection of the inner and outer forces that make me who I am, converging in the irreducible mystery of being human.

By *integrity* I mean whatever wholeness I am able to find within that nexus as its vectors form and re-form the pattern of my life. Integrity requires that I discern what is integral to my selfhood, what fits and what does not—and that I choose life-giving ways of relating to the forces that converge within me: do I welcome them or fear them, embrace them or reject them, move with them or against them? By choosing integrity I become more whole, but wholeness does not mean perfection. It means becoming more real by acknowledging the whole of who I am.

Identity and integrity are not the granite from which fictional heroes are hewn. They are subtle dimensions of the complex, demanding, and life-long process of self-discovery. *Identity* lies in the intersection of the diverse forces that make up my life, and *integrity* lies in relating to those forces in ways that bring me wholeness and life rather than fragmentation and death.

Those are my definitions—but try as I may to refine them, they always come out too pat. Identity and integrity can never be fully named or known by anyone, including the person who bears them. They constitute that familiar strangeness we take with us to the grave, elusive realities that can be caught only occasionally out of the corner of the eye.

Stories are the best way to portray realities of this sort, so here is a tale of two teachers—a tale based on people I have known, whose lives tell me more about the subtleties of identity and integrity than any theory could.

Alan and Eric were born into two different families of skilled crafts people, rural folk with little formal schooling but gifted in the manual arts. Both boys evinced this gift from childhood onward, and as each grew in the skill at working with his hands, each developed a sense of self in which the pride of craft was key.

The two shared another gift as well: both excelled in school and became the first in their working-class families to go to college. Both did well as undergraduates, both were admitted to graduate school, both earned doctorates, and both chose academic careers.

But here their paths diverged. Though the gift of craft was central in both men's sense of self, Alan was able to weave that gift into his academic vocation while the fabric of Eric's life unraveled early on.

Catapulted from his rural community into an elite private college at age eighteen, Eric suffered severe culture shock—and never overcame it. He was insecure with fellow students and, later, with academic colleagues who came from backgrounds he saw as more "cultured" than his own. He learned to speak and act like an intellectual, but he always felt fraudulent among people who were, in his eyes, to the manor born.

But insecurity neither altered Eric's course nor drew him into self-reflection. Instead, he bullied his way into professional life on the theory that the best defense is a good offense. He made pronouncements rather than probes. He listened for weaknesses rather than strengths in what other people said. He argued with anyone about anything—and responded with veiled contempt to whatever was said in return.

In the classroom, Eric was critical and judgmental, quick to put down the "stupid question," adept at trapping students with trick questions of his own, then merciless in mocking wrong answers. He seemed driven by a need to inflict upon his students the same wound that academic life had inflicted upon him—the wound of being embarrassed by some essential part of one's self.

But when Eric went home to his workbench and lost himself in craft, he found himself as well. He became warm and welcoming, at home in the world and glad to extend hospitality to others.

Reconnected with his roots, centered in his true self, he was able to reclaim a quiet and confident core—which he quickly lost as soon as he returned to campus.

Alan's is a different story. His leap from countryside to campus did not induce culture shock, in part because he attended a land-grant university where many students had backgrounds much like his own. He was not driven to hide his gift, but was able to honor and transform it by turning it toward things academic: he brought to his study, and later to his teaching and research, the same sense of craft that his ancestors brought to their work with metal and wood.

Watching Alan teach, you felt that you were watching a crafts-man at work—and if you knew his history, you understood that this feeling was more than metaphor. In his lectures, every move Alan made was informed by attention to detail and respect for the mate-rials at hand; he connected ideas with the precision of dovetail join-ery and finished the job with a polished summary.

But the power of Alan's teaching went well beyond crafted per-formance. His students knew that Alan would extend himself with great generosity to any of them who wanted to become an appren-tice in his field, just as the elders in his own family had extended themselves to help young Alan grow in his original craft.

Alan taught from an undivided self—the integral state of being which is central to good teaching. In the undivided self, every major thread of one's life experience is honored, creating a weave of such coherence and strength that it can hold students and subject as well as self. Such a self, inwardly integrated, is able to make the outward connections on which good teaching depends.

But Eric failed to weave the central strand of his identity into his academic vocation. His was a self divided, engaged in a civil war. He projected that inner warfare onto the outer world, and his teach-ing devolved into combat instead of craft. The divided self will always distance itself from others, and may even try to destroy them, to defend its fragile identity.

If Eric had not been alienated as an undergraduate—or if his alienation had led to self-reflection instead of self-defense—it is pos-sible that he, like Alan, could have found integrity in his academic vocation, could have woven the major strands of his identity into his

APPENDIX B

work. But part of the mystery of selfhood is the fact that one size does not fit all: what is integral to one person lacks integrity for another. Throughout his life there were persistent clues that academia was not a life-giving choice for Eric, not a context in which his true self could emerge healthy and whole, not a vocation integral to his unique nature.

The self is not infinitely elastic—it has potentials and it has limits. If the work we do lacks integrity for us, then we, the work, and the people we do it with will suffer. Alan's self was enlarged by his academic vocation, and the work he did was a joy to behold. Eric's self was diminished by his encounter with academia, and choosing a different vocation might have been his only way to recover integrity lost.

When Teachers Lose Heart

As good teachers weave the fabric that joins them with students and subjects, the heart is the loom on which the threads are tied, the tension is held, the shuttle flies, and the fabric is stretched tight. Small wonder, then, that teaching tugs at the heart, opens the heart, even breaks the heart—and the more one loves teaching, the more heartbreaking it can be.

We became teachers for reasons of the heart, animated by a passion for some subject and for helping people to learn. But many of us lose heart as the years of teaching go by. How can we take heart in teaching once more, so we can do what good teachers always do—give heart to our students? The courage to teach is the courage to keep one's heart open in those very moments when the heart is asked to hold more than it is able, so that teacher and students and subject can be woven into the fabric of community that learning, and living, require.

There are no techniques for reclaiming our hearts, for keeping our hearts open. Indeed, the heart does not seek "fixes" but insight and understanding. When we lose heart, we need an understanding of our condition that will liberate us from that condition, a diagnosis that will lead us toward new ways of being in the classroom simply by telling the truth about who, and how, we are. Truth, not technique, is what heals and empowers the heart.

We lose heart, in part, because teaching is a daily exercise in vulnerability. I need not reveal personal secrets to feel naked in front of a class. I need only parse a sentence or work a proof on the board while my students doze off or pass notes. No matter how technical or abstract my subject may be, the things I teach are things I care about—and what I care about helps define my selfhood.

Unlike many professions, teaching is always done at the dangerous intersection of personal and public life. A good therapist must work in a personal way, but never publicly: the therapist who reveals as much as a client's name is derelict. A good trial lawyer must work in a public forum, but unswayed by personal opinion: the lawyer who allows his or her feelings about a client's guilt to weaken the client's defense is guilty of malpractice.

But a good teacher must stand where personal and public meet, dealing with the thundering flow of traffic at an intersection where "weaving a web of connectedness" feels more like crossing a freeway on foot. As we try to connect ourselves and our subjects with our students, we make ourselves, as well as our subjects, vulnerable to indifference, judgment, ridicule.

To reduce our vulnerability, we disconnect from students, from subjects, and even from ourselves. We build a wall between inner truth and outer performance, and we play-act the teacher's part. Our words, spoken at remove from our hearts, become "the balloon speech in cartoons," and we become caricatures of ourselves. We distance ourselves from students and subject to minimize the danger—forgetting that distance makes life more dangerous still by isolating the self.

This self-protective split of personhood from practice is encouraged by an academic culture that distrusts personal truth. Though the academy claims to value multiple modes of knowing, it honors only one—an "objective" way of knowing that takes us into the "real" world by taking us "out of ourselves."

In this culture, objective facts are regarded as pure while subjective feelings are suspect and sullied. In this culture, the self is not a source to be tapped but a danger to be suppressed, not a potential to be fulfilled but an obstacle to be overcome. In this culture, the pathology of speech disconnected from self is regarded, and rewarded, as a virtue.

If my sketch of the academic bias against selfhood seems overdone, here is another story from my own teaching experience. I assigned my students a series of brief analytical essays involving themes in the texts we were going to be reading. Then I assigned a parallel series of autobiographical sketches, related to those themes, so my students could see connections between the textbook concepts and their own lives.

After the first class, a student spoke to me: "In those autobiographical essays you asked us to write, is it okay to use the word 'I'?"

I did not know whether to laugh or cry—but I knew that my response would have considerable impact on a young man who had just opened himself to ridicule. I told him that not only could he use the word "I," but I hoped he would use it freely and often. Then I asked what had led to his question.

"I'm a history major," he said, "and each time I use 'I' in a paper, they knock off half a grade."

The academic bias against subjectivity not only forces our students to write poorly ("It is believed . . ." instead of "I believe . . ."), it deforms their thinking about themselves and their world. In a single stroke, we delude our students into believing that bad prose turns opinions into facts and we alienate them from their own inner lives.

Faculty often complain that students have no regard for the gifts of insight and understanding that are the true payoff of education— they care only about short-term outcomes in the "real" world: "Will this major get me a job?" "How will this assignment be useful in 'real' life?"

But those are not the questions deep in our students' hearts. They are merely the questions they have been taught to ask, not only by tuition-paying parents who want their children to be employable, but by an academic culture that distrusts and devalues inner reality. Of course our students are cynical about the inner outcomes of education: we teach them that the subjective self is irrelevant and even unreal.

The foundation of any culture lies in the way it answers the question, "Where do reality and power reside?" For some cultures the answer is the gods, for some it is nature, for some it is tradition. In our culture, the answer is clear: reality and power reside in the external world of objects and events, and in the sciences that study that world, while the inner realm of "heart" is a romantic fantasy— an escape from harsh realities perhaps, but surely not a source of leverage over "the real world."

We are obsessed with manipulating externals because we believe that they will give us some power over reality and win us some freedom from its constraints. Mesmerized by a technology that seems to done just that, we dismiss the inward world. We turn every question we face into an objective problem to be solved—and we believe that for every objective problem there is some sort of technical fix.

That is why we train doctors to repair the body but not to honor the spirit; clergy to be CEO's but not spiritual guides; teachers to master techniques but not to engage their students' hearts—or their own. That is why our students are cynical about the efficacy of an education that transforms the inner landscape of their lives: when academic culture dismisses inner truth and pays homage only to the objective world, students as well as teachers lose heart.

LISTENING TO THE TEACHER WITHIN

Recovering the heart to teach requires us to reclaim our relationship with the teacher within. This teacher is one whom we knew when we were children but lost touch with as we grew into adulthood, a teacher who continually invites me to honor my true self—not my ego or expectations or image or role, but the self I am when all the externals are stripped away.

By inner teacher, I do not mean "conscience" or "superego," moral arbiter or internalized judge. In fact, conscience, as it is commonly understood, can get us into deep vocational trouble. When we listen primarily for what we "ought" to be doing with our lives, we may find ourselves hounded by external expectations that can distort our identity and integrity. There is much that I "ought" to be doing by some abstract moral calculus. But is it my vocation? Am I gifted and called to do it? Is this particular "ought" a place of intersection between my inner self and the outer world, or is it someone else's image of how my life should look?

When I follow only the oughts, I may find myself doing work that is ethically laudable but that is not mine to do. A vocation that is not mine, no matter how externally valued, does violence to the self—in the precise sense that it *violates* my identity and integrity on behalf of some abstract norm. When I violate myself, I invariably end up violating the people I work with. How many teachers inflict their own pain on their students, the pain that comes from doing a work that never was, or no longer is, their true work?

The teacher within is not the voice of conscience but of identity and integrity. It speaks not of what ought to be, but of what is real for us, of what is true. It says things like, "This is what fits you and this is what doesn't." "This is who you are and this is who you are not." "This is what gives you life and this is what kills your spirit—or makes you wish you were dead." The teacher within stands guard at the gate of selfhood, warding off whatever insults our integrity and welcoming whatever affirms it. The voice of the inward teacher reminds me of my potentials and limits as I negotiate the force-field of my life.

I realize that the idea of a "teacher within" strikes some academics as a romantic fantasy, but I cannot fathom why. If there is no such reality in our lives, centuries of Western discourse about the aims of education become so much lip-flapping. In classical understanding, education is the attempt to "lead out" from within the self a core of wisdom that has the power to resist falsehood and live in the light of truth, not by external norms but by reasoned and reflective self-determination. The inward teacher is the living core of our lives that is addressed and evoked by any education worthy of the name.

Perhaps the idea is unpopular because it compels us to look at two of the most difficult truths about teaching. The first is that what we teach will never "take" unless it connects with the inward, living core of our students' lives, with our students' inward teachers.

We can, and do, make education an exclusively outward enterprise, forcing students to memorize and repeat facts without ever appealing to their inner truth—and we get predictable results: many students never want to read a challenging book or think a creative thought once they get out of school. The kind of teaching that transforms people does not happen if the student's inward teacher is ignored.

The second truth is even more daunting: we can speak to the teacher within our students only when we are on speaking terms with the teacher within ourselves.

The student who said that her bad teachers spoke like cartoon characters was describing teachers who have grown deaf to their inner guide, who have so thoroughly separated inner truth from outer actions that they have lost touch with a sense of self. Deep speaks to deep, and when we have not sounded our own depths, we cannot sound the depths of our students' lives.

How does one attend to the voice of the teacher within? I have no particular methods to suggest, other than the familiar ones: solitude and silence, meditative reading and walking in the woods, keeping a journal, finding a friend who will simply listen. I merely propose that we need to learn as many ways as we can of "talking to ourselves."

That phrase, of course, is one we normally use to name a symptom of mental imbalance—a clear sign of how our culture regards the idea of an inner voice! But people who learn to talk to themselves may soon delight in the discovery that the teacher within is the sanest conversation partner they have ever had.

We need to find every possible way to listen to that voice and take its counsel seriously, not only for the sake of our work, but for the sake of our own health. If someone in the outer world is trying to tell us something important and we ignore his or her presence, that person either gives up and stops speaking or becomes more and more violent in attempting to get our attention.

Similarly, if we do not respond to the voice of the inward teacher, it will either stop speaking or become violent: I am convinced that some forms of depression, of which I have personal experience, are induced by a long-ignored inner teacher trying desperately to get us to listen by threatening to destroy us. When we honor that voice with simple attention, it responds by speaking more gently and engaging us in a life-giving conversation of the soul.

That conversation does not have to reach conclusions in order to be of value: we do not need to emerge from "talking to ourselves" with clear goals, objectives, and plans. Measuring the value of inner dialogue by its practical outcomes is like measuring the value of a friendship by the number of problems that are solved when friends get together.

Conversation among friends has its own rewards: in the presence of our friends we have the simple joy of feeling at ease, at home, trusted and able to trust. We attend to the inner teacher not to get fixed but to befriend the deeper self, to cultivate a sense of identity and integrity that allows us to feel at home wherever we are.

Listening to the inner teacher also offers an answer to one of the most basic questions teachers face: how can I develop the *authority* to teach, the capacity to stand my ground in the midst of the complex forces of both the classroom and my own life?

In a culture of objectification and technique we often confuse authority with power, but the two are not the same. Power works from the outside in, but authority works from the inside out. We are mistaken when we seek "authority" outside ourselves, in sources ranging from the subtle skills of group process to that less-than-subtle method of social control called grading. This view of teaching turns the teacher into the cop on the corner, trying to keep things moving amicably and by consent, but always having recourse to the coercive power of the law.

External tools of power have occasional utility in teaching, but they are no substitute for authority, the authority that comes from the teacher's inner life. The clue is in the word itself, which has "author" at its core. Authority is granted to people who are perceived as "authoring" their own words, their own actions, their own lives, rather than playing a scripted role at great remove from their own hearts. When teachers depend on the coercive powers of law or technique, they have no authority at all.

I am painfully aware of the times in my own teaching when I lose touch with my inner teacher, and therefore with my own authority. In those times I try to gain power by barricading myself behind the podium and my status while wielding the threat of grades. But when my teaching is authorized by the teacher within me, I need neither weapons nor armor to teach.

Authority comes as I reclaim my identity and integrity, remembering my selfhood and my sense of vocation. Then teaching can come from the depths of my own truth—and the truth that is within my students has a chance to respond in kind.

INSTITUTIONS AND THE HUMAN HEART

My concern for the "inner landscape" of teaching may seem indulgent, even irrelevant, at a time when many teachers are struggling simply to survive. Wouldn't it be more practical, I am sometimes asked, to offer tips, tricks, and techniques for staying alive in the classroom, things that ordinary teachers can use in everyday life?

I have worked with countless teachers, and many of them have confirmed my own experience: as important as methods may be, the most practical thing we can achieve in any kind of work is insight into what is happening inside us as we do it. The more familiar we are with our inner terrain, the more sure-footed our teaching—and living—becomes.

I have heard that in the training of therapists, which involves much practical technique, there is a saying: "Technique is what you use until the therapist arrives." Good methods can help a therapist find a way into the client's dilemma, but good therapy does not begin until the real-life therapist joins with the real life of the client.

Technique is what teachers use until the real teacher arrives, and we need to find as many ways as possible to help that teacher show up. But if we want to develop the identity and integrity that good teaching requires, we must do something alien to academic culture: we must talk to each other about our inner lives, risky stuff in a profession that fears the personal and seeks safety in the technical, the distant, the abstract.

I was reminded of that fear recently as I listened to a group of faculty argue about what to do when students share personal experiences in class—experiences that are related to the themes of the course, but that some professors regard as "more suited to a therapy session than to a college classroom."

The house soon divided along predictable lines. On one side were the scholars, insisting that the subject is primary and must never be compromised for the sake of the students' lives. On the other side were the student-centered folks, insisting that the lives of students must always come first even if it means that the subject gets short-changed. The more vigorously these camps promoted their polarized ideas, the more antagonistic they became—and the less they learned about pedagogy or about themselves.

The gap between these views seems unbridgeable—until we understand what creates it. At bottom, these professors were not debating teaching techniques. They were revealing the diversity of identity and integrity among themselves, saying, in various ways, "Here are my own limits and potentials when it comes to dealing with the relation between the subject and my students' lives."

If we stopped lobbing pedagogical points at each other and spoke about *who we are* as teachers, a remarkable thing might happen: identity and integrity might grow within us and among us, instead of hardening as they do when we defend our fixed positions from the foxholes of the pedagogy wars.

But telling the truth about ourselves with colleagues in the workplace is an enterprise fraught with danger, against which we have erected formidable taboos. We fear making ourselves vulnerable in the midst of competitive people and politics that could easily turn against us, and we claim the inalienable right to separate the "personal" and the "professional" into airtight compartments (even though everyone knows the two are inseparably intertwined). So we keep the workplace conversation objective and external, finding it safer to talk about technique than about selfhood.

Indeed, the story I most often hear from faculty (and other professionals) is that the institutions in which they work are the heart's worst enemy. In this story, institutions continually try to diminish the human heart in order to consolidate their own power, and the individual is left with a discouraging choice: to distance one's self from the institution and its mission and sink into deepening cynicism (an occupational hazard of academic life), or to maintain eternal vigilance against institutional invasion and fight for one's life when it comes.

Taking the conversation of colleagues into the deep places where we might grow in self-knowledge for the sake of our professional practice will not be an easy, or popular, task. But it is a task that leaders of every educational institution must take up if they wish to strengthen their institution's capacity to pursue the educational mission. How can schools educate students if they fail to support the teacher's inner life? To educate is to guide students on an inner journey toward more truthful ways of seeing and being in the world. How can schools perform their mission without encouraging the guides to scout out that inner terrain?

As this century of objectification and manipulation by technique draws to a close, we are experiencing an exhaustion of institutional resourcefulness at the very time when the problems that our institutions must address grow deeper and more demanding. Just as twentieth century medicine, famous for its externalized fixes for disease, has found itself required to reach deeper for the psychological and spiritual dimensions of healing, so twentieth century education must open up a new frontier in teaching and learning—the frontier of the teacher's inner life.

How this might be done is a subject I have explored in earlier essays in *Change,* so I will not repeat myself here. In "Good Talk About Good Teaching," I examined some of the key elements necessary for an institution to host non-compulsory, non-invasive opportunities for faculty to help themselves and each other grow inwardly as teachers.[1] In "Divided No More: A Movement Approach to Educational Reform," I explored things we can do on our own when institutions are resistant or hostile to the inner agenda.[2]

Our task is to create enough safe spaces and trusting relationships within the academic workplace—hedged about by appropriate structural protections—that more of us will be able to tell the truth about our own struggles and joys as teachers in ways that befriend the soul and give it room to grow. Not all spaces can be safe, not all relationships trustworthy, but we can surely develop more of them than we now have so that an increase of honesty and healing can happen within us and among us—for our own sake, the sake of our teaching, and the sake of our students.

Honesty and healing sometimes happen quite simply, thanks to the alchemical powers of the human soul. When I, with thirty years of teaching experience, speak openly about the fact that I still approach each new class with trepidation, younger faculty tell me that this makes their own fears seem more natural—and thus easier to transcend—and a rich dialogue about the teacher's selfhood often ensues. We do not discuss techniques for "fear management," if such exist. Instead, we meet as fellow travelers and offer encouragement to each other in this demanding but deeply rewarding journey across the inner landscape of education—calling each other back to the identity and integrity that animate all good work, not least the work called teaching.

NOTES

1. "Good Talk About Good Teaching: Improving Teaching Through Conversation and Community," *Change,* Nov.-Dec., 1993. A revised version of this article appears as Chapter VI in *The Courage to Teach.*
2. "Divided No More: A Movement Approach to Educational Reform," *Change,* Mar.-Apr. 1992. A revised version of this article appears as Chapter VII in *The Courage to Teach.*

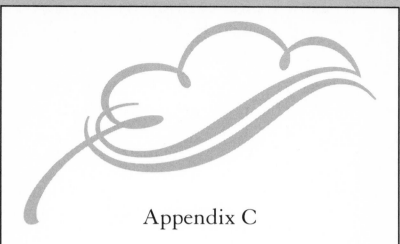

Appendix C

The Clearness Committee

A Communal Approach to Discernment

This material was originally published as Chapter VIII, "Living the Questions: Experiments with Truth," in Parker J. Palmer, *A Hidden Wholeness: The Journey Toward an Undivided Life* (San Francisco: Jossey-Bass, 2004).

> Be patient toward all that is unsolved in your heart and
> try to love the questions themselves. . . . Live the questions now.
> Perhaps you will then gradually, without noticing it,
> live along some distant day into the answer.
> RAINER MARIA RILKE, *Letters to a Young Poet*

THE TRUTH BENEATH MY FEAR

If we want to create a space that welcomes the soul, we must speak our own truth to the center of the circle and listen receptively as others speak theirs. We must also respond to what others say in ways that extend the welcome, something that rarely happens in daily life.

Listen in on conventional conversations and see how often we respond to each other by agreeing, disagreeing, or simply changing the subject! We do not mean to be inhospitable to the soul, and yet we often are. By inserting our opinions and asserting our agendas, we advance our egos while the speaker's inner teacher retreats.

In a circle of trust, we learn an alternative way to respond, centered on the rare art of asking honest, open questions—questions that invite a speaker to reach for deeper and truer speech. If you do not believe that such questions are rare, just count how many you are asked over the next few days. Honest, open questions are countercultural, but they are vital to a circle of trust. Such questions, asked in a safe space, invite the inner teacher to say more about the matter at hand. And they give the speaker a chance to hear that voice free of the static we create by imposing our predilections on each other.

A few years ago, I became aware of my own need for another talk with the inner teacher. I had entered my early sixties and was feeling anxious about the future, for reasons I did not understand. So I invited a few friends to help me discern what my feelings meant.

The people I called on were experienced and wise, but I did not need their opinions or advice. I needed them to ask me honest, open

 SEGMENT 24: THE CLEARNESS COMMITTEE

To learn more about this process, view Segment 24 on the DVD that accompanies this *Guide*.

questions in the hope that I could touch the truth beneath my fear. Guided by the ground rules described in this chapter, they did just that for me. In three two-hour gatherings over a period of eighteen months, they created a space where I was able to discover the source of my anxiety.

Slowly, and with some reluctance, I began to see that what I feared was the impending collision of my age, vocation, and survival. I have worked independently since my late forties, earning my living partly by writing but largely by lecturing and leading workshops around the country. Now, in my early sixties—as I looked down the road at an endless procession of airports, hotel rooms, restaurant food, and auditoriums full of strangers—I worried about my diminishing stamina for this kind of work and about my diminishing income if I were to lay it down.

I was stuck on the horns of that dilemma until the third gathering of my group. I made some comment about aging and fear, and someone responded, "What do you fear most about growing old?" This was not the first time I had been asked that question; in fact, the question was one that I had often asked myself. But this time, my answer came from a place deeper than ego or intellect, in words I had never spoken or even thought: "I fear becoming a seventy-year-old man who does not know who he is when the books are out of print and the audiences are no longer applauding."

The moment I heard those words, I knew I had heard my soul speak—and I knew that I had to act on what I had heard. At stake was not merely my physical and financial comfort but my sense of identity and my spiritual well-being. So I began creating a retirement plan that I am now living into. It is a plan that gives me an opportunity to find out who else might be "in here" besides a writer and a speaker and to act on whatever I may learn while I still have energy and time.

LEARNING TO ASK

I could not have made this decision, with all its attendant risks, without a small group of people whose honest, open questions created a space that invited my soul to speak and allowed me to hear it.

Such questioning may sound easy. But many people, including me, have trouble framing questions that are not advice in disguise. "Have you thought about seeing a therapist?" is *not* an honest, open question! A question like that serves my needs, not yours, pressing you toward my version of your problem and its solution instead of evoking your truth. Many of us need help learning how to ask questions that make the shy soul want to speak up, not shut up.

What are the marks of an honest, open question? An *honest* question is one I can ask without possibly being able to say to myself, "I know the right answer to this question, and I sure hope you give it to me"—which is, of course, what I am doing when I ask you about seeing a therapist. A dishonest question insults your soul, partly because of my arrogance in assuming that I know what you need and partly because of my fraudulence in trying to disguise my counsel as a query.

When I ask you an honest question—for example, "Have you ever had an experience that felt like your current dilemma?" or "Did you learn anything from that prior experience that feels useful to you now?"—there is no way for me to imagine what the "right answer" might be. Your soul feels welcome to speak its truth in response to questions like these because they harbor no hidden agendas.

An *open* question is one that expands rather than restricts your arena of exploration, one that does not push or even nudge you toward a particular way of framing a situation. "How do you feel about the experience you just described?" is an open question. "Why do you seem so sad?" is not.

We all know the difference between open and closed questions, and yet we often slip-slide toward the latter. For example, as I listen to you answer an open question about how you feel, I realize that you have not mentioned anger. Barely aware of what I am doing, I start thinking to myself, "If I were in your situation, I would certainly feel angry . . ."; then I think, "You must be bottling your anger up, and that's not good . . ."; and so I ask you, "Do you feel any anger?"

That question may seem open, since it allows you to answer any way you wish. But because it is driven by my desire to suggest how you *ought* to feel, it is likely to scare your soul away. The fact that I would be angry if I were in your shoes does not mean you have hidden anger; as hard as I may find it to believe, not everyone's inner life is the same as mine! And if you do have hidden anger, my effort to draw it out is likely to make you bury it deeper, as a protection against my presumptuousness. If you are angry, you will deal with it on your timetable, not mine—and step one will be to name your anger for yourself rather than accept my naming of it.

"Try not to get ahead of the language a speaker uses" is a good guideline for asking honest, open questions. By paying close attention to the words people speak, we can ask questions that invite them to probe what they may already know but have not yet fully named. If I ask you, "What did you mean when you said you felt 'frustrated'?" it might help you discover other feelings—if they are there and if you are ready to name them.

But even a question like that will shut you down if I ask it in the hope of getting you to "say the magic word," such as *anger,* that I am expecting to hear! The soul is a highly tuned bunk detector. It is quick to register, and flee from, all attempts at manipulation.

In my own struggle to learn to ask honest, open questions, I find it helpful to have a few guidelines. But the best way to make sure that my questions will welcome the soul is to ask them with an honest, open spirit. And the best way to cultivate that spirit is to remind myself regularly that everyone has an inner teacher whose authority in his or her life far exceeds my own.

The finest school I know for watching the inner teacher at work and learning to ask honest, open questions is a discernment process called the "clearness committee" that has become standard practice in many circles of trust. That name makes it sound like something that came from the sixties, and so it did—the 1660s!

The clearness committee (so named because it helps us achieve clarity) was invented by the early Quakers. As a church that chose to do without benefit of ordained clergy, Quakers needed a structure to help members deal with problems that people in other denominations would simply take to their pastors or priests. That structure had to embody two key Quaker convictions: our guidance comes not from external authority but from the inner teacher, and we need community to help us clarify and amplify the inner teacher's voice.

Appendix C

The clearness committee that resulted is not just a place where we learn to ask honest, open questions. It is a focused microcosm of a larger circle of trust, a setting in which we have an intense experience of what it means to gather in support of someone's inner journey. When clearness committees become a regular part of an ongoing circle of trust, everything else that happens in the circle gains depth—which is why the rest of this chapter is devoted to explaining the clearness process.

GAINING CLARITY

The process begins with a "focus person"—someone who is wrestling with an issue related to his or her personal life or work (or both)—inviting four to six people to serve on his or her committee.

"Four to six" is not a casual suggestion: a clearness committee works best with no fewer than four people and no more than six, in addition to the focus person. They should, of course, be people whom the focus person trusts, and when possible, they should represent a variety of backgrounds, experiences, and viewpoints.[1]

Normally, the focus person writes a two- or three-page statement of the problem and gives it to committee members before they meet. If writing does not come easily to the focus person, he or she can tape-record some reflections to share with the committee in advance or make some notes to guide an oral presentation of the problem when the committee gathers.

As a first step toward "clearness," people usually find it helpful to frame the presentation of their problem in three parts:

• *Identifying the problem, as best one is able.* Sometimes the problem is clear ("I have a choice between two job offers"), and sometimes it is vague ("Something is off-center in my life, but I am not really sure what it is"). Since clarity is the aim of the process, the problem itself can be, and often is, murky. And even when the problem seems clear to the focus person, the process may reveal that the real problem is something else!

- *Offering background information that bears directly on the problem.* A modest amount of autobiographical information can help move a clearness committee along. If, for example, you are thinking about leaving your job and you have changed jobs five times in the past decade, you would do well to offer this fact up front.
- *Naming whatever clues there may be on the horizon about where you are headed with the problem.* Here the focus person shares any hunches he or she may have about the issue at hand—whether it is an inclination toward one of those two job offers or simply an anxious feeling about the foggy vista up ahead.

Before the clearness committee begins, members spend some time with the focus person reviewing the rules that govern the process, which will be explained as this chapter proceeds. It is important that everyone understand the rules—as well as the principles behind them—and take seriously the obligation that comes with promising to hold safe space for someone's soul.

Members of the committee should have a printed schedule, modeled on the one presented here, to help them keep the time as well as the rules. Even when the process feels sluggish or the focus person's problem seems to have been resolved, staying with the schedule often yields unexpected insights. So the total time of two hours is nonnegotiable, as is the amount of time allotted for each portion of the process:

7:00 P.M.	Sit down in silence in a circle of chairs. The silence will be broken by the focus person when he or she is ready to begin.
7:00–7:15	The focus person describes his or her issue while committee members listen, without interruption.
7:15–8:45	Questions only! For an hour and a half, members of the committee may not speak to the focus person in any way except to ask brief, honest, open questions.
8:45–8:55	Does the focus person want members to "mirror back" what they have heard—in addition to asking more questions—or to continue with questions only?

Appendix C

	If mirroring is invited, members are to reflect the focus person's words or body language, without interpretation.
8:55–9:00	Affirmations and celebrations of the focus person, each other, and the shared experience.
9:00 P.M.	End—remembering to honor the rule of "double confidentiality."

The clearness committee begins with several minutes of silence, which is broken by the focus person when he or she is ready to present the problem. Even when the problem has been shared with committee members in advance, this oral review often reveals nuances that can be conveyed only face to face. The presentation should take no more than fifteen minutes, and during that time, members may not speak, even to ask for clarification.

When the focus person is finished presenting the problem, he or she lets the group members know that their work can begin. For the next ninety minutes, committee members are guided by a simple but demanding rule: *the only way they may speak to the focus person is to ask brief, honest, open questions.*

The questions should be short and to the point, confined to a single sentence, if possible. When I ask a question by saying, "You mentioned such-and-such, which made me think of such-and-such, and so I'd like to ask you such-and-such . . . ," I am often trying to nudge the focus person toward my way of looking at things. A brief question, with no preamble or explanation, reduces the risk that I will start to offer covert advice.

The questions should be gently paced, with periods of silence between a question, a response, and the next question. The clearness committee is not a grilling or a cross-examination; a relaxed and graceful pace helps the shy soul feel safe. If I ask the focus person one question and, after he or she has answered, follow up with another, it is probably all right. But if I am tempted to ask a third question before anyone else has had a chance, I need to take a deep breath and remember that there are other people in the room.

I should not ask questions simply to satisfy my curiosity. Instead, my questions should come from a desire to support the focus person's inner journey with as much purity as I can muster. As a member of the committee, I am not here to get my own needs met. I am here to be fully present to the focus person, hoping to help that person be fully present to his or her soul.

It is usually most helpful to ask questions that are more about the person than about the problem, since a clearness committee is less about problem solving than about drawing close to true self. I remember a committee called by a CEO who was dealing with a complex and painful racial issue in her corporation. She found it helpful when one member asked, "What have you learned about yourself in previous conflicts that might be useful to you now?" But she found it unhelpful when another asked, "Do you have a good corporate lawyer?"

If the focus person feels that a question is not honest and open, he or she has the right to say so, to call a questioner back to the rules and the spirit behind them. But if my question is found wanting, I do *not* have the right to explain or defend myself: "You see, that question came to me when you said such-and-such, then I thought such-and-such, and what I really meant was such-and-such."

Such an "explanation" is just one more way of trying to nudge the focus person toward my way of thinking. If I am challenged by the focus person, I have only one option: to sit back, absorb the critique, and eventually return to the process in a more helpful way. Offering any sort of explanation or defense puts my needs and interests ahead of the focus person's and will scare off his or her soul.

Normally, as questions are asked, the focus person answers them aloud, which helps the person hear whatever the inner teacher is saying. But the focus person has the right to pass on any question, without explanation, and committee members should avoid asking questions of a similar sort. Taking a pass does not mean that the focus person is stifling the inner teacher: he or she may learn something important from the fact that a certain question cannot be answered in front of other people.

No One to Fool but Myself

The discipline of asking honest, open questions is the heart of the clearness committee. But there are other disciplines that guide the committee's work, all of them aimed at supporting the focus person on his or her inner journey.

If the focus person cries, committee members are not free to offer "comfort" by giving the person a tissue, laying a hand on his or her shoulder, or speaking words of consolation. Acts such as these may be compassionate under normal circumstances, but they are disruptive in a clearness committee.

If I try to comfort the focus person, I take his or her attention away from whatever message may be in those tears. Now the focus person is attending to *me*—not the inner teacher—trying to make me feel like a good caregiver: "Thank you for your concern. But please, don't worry about me. I'll be OK. . . ." By engaging the focus person in an interpersonal exchange, I have derailed his or her inner journey. I must remember that for these two hours, I have only one responsibility: to help the focus person devote undivided attention to the voice of true self.

By the same token, if the focus person cracks a good joke, I am not free to laugh long and loud, though a soft smile will do no harm. Once again, behavior that we normally regard as supportive is disruptive and distracting in this setting. By joining the focus person in laughter, I not only call attention to myself—"See, I have a sense of humor too!"—but I may also prevent the focus person from asking a critical inner question: "Am I using my sense of humor to cover up the pain I felt when that question was asked?"

One of the most demanding disciplines of a clearness committee involves eye contact. In our culture, it is generally regarded as impolite *not* to look each other in the eye when we talk. But observe what happens the next time you are in a conversation involving several people. As one person speaks, the listeners send silent signals—smiling and nodding, cocking their heads, furrowing their brows.

They give the speaker a steady stream of clues about whether they understand or appreciate whatever he or she is saying.

These clues are meant to be helpful, and so they can be, *if* the speaker's goal is to persuade or connect with other people. But nonverbal clues usually nudge the speaker down a path chosen partly by the listeners, rather than one dictated exclusively by the speaker's inner teacher. As we pick up these signals from others, we often alter what we are saying in the hope of achieving our rhetorical goal.

In a clearness committee, the focus person's goal is to communicate with true self, not with other people. Here nonverbal signals are not just irrelevant; they can easily lead the person down a false path. What committee members think or feel about what a focus person says is of no consequence. The only responses that count are those that come from within the focus person.

So members of a clearness committee try to refrain from nonverbal responses and to listen to the focus person with as much receptive neutrality as they can muster. But most of us find it very hard to achieve this state. So the focus person is encouraged to break eye contact when answering a questions, or even for the full two hours—to speak with eyes closed or cast down to the floor—in order to avoid seeing the nonverbal signals that committee members may be sending.

At first, the focus person may find it as hard to break eye contact as the committee members find it to withhold nonverbal responses. But after a while, these practices become liberating for everyone. They encourage truthful speaking and receptive listening, drawing us deep into a space that honors and welcomes the soul.

For thirty years, I have used clearness committees to help me make important decisions. As I have listened to people's honest, open questions—and to my inner teacher's response—I have always had the same thought: in this space, I don't need to convince anyone of anything, so there's no one left to fool except myself. In this moment, nothing makes sense except to speak my own truth as clearly as I know how. That simple realization has allowed me to hear, and follow, some inner imperatives that have changed the course of my life.

CAUSE FOR CELEBRATION

After an hour and a half of questions and responses, the clearness committee enters its final phase. With fifteen minutes remaining, someone asks the focus person if he or she would like members to "mirror back" what they have heard, in addition to asking more questions, or would prefer to continue with the "questions only" rule.

As a focus person, I have always chosen mirroring, because new insights often come to me in that final phase of the process. But because mirroring releases members from the "questions only" rule, it puts us on the edge of a slippery slope where we might start trying to fix, save, advise, or set the focus person straight. So mirroring is protected by clear definitions of what is and is not allowed: it can take three, and only three, forms.

The first involves saying to the focus person, "When you were asked such-and-such a question, you gave such-and-such an answer . . ."—with both the question and the answer being direct quotes, not paraphrases, of what was said. Obviously, if I hold up such a mirror, I think there is something in that question and answer that the focus person needs to see. But I am not allowed to say what that something is, lest I start offering advice. The focus person is free to speak, or not, about the reflection I offer: what matters is not what I see in the focus person's words but what the focus person sees in them as I mirror them back.

The second form of mirroring involves quoting two or three answers the focus person gave to two or three different questions, inviting the person to look at them in relation to one another. By "connecting the dots" in a way that suggests a pattern among the answers, I am coming dangerously close to analyzing the problem and perhaps even proposing a "solution." But again, I am not allowed to describe or even hint at the pattern I think I see. And again, the focus person is free to respond in any way he or she wishes, including saying nothing at all.

The third form of mirroring involves the focus person's body language. I might say to the focus person, "When you were asked about the job offer from the insurance company, you slumped in your chair and spoke in a soft monotone. When you were asked about the offer from the National Park Service, you sat up straight and spoke louder and with inflection."

It is critical that I *describe* rather than *interpret* body language. "You slumped in your chair and spoke in a soft monotone" is a description. "You seemed unenthusiastic, even depressed, as you spoke" is an interpretation. The former allows the focus person to look into the mirror and come to his or her own conclusions about what is there; the latter is a judgment that may create resistance, not receptivity. And my judgment may well be wrong. A posture that says "depressed" to me may reflect deep thoughtfulness in the speaker.

Body language is usually inaudible to the person who "speaks" it. So despite the ever-present slippery slope, mirroring it back in a purely reflective manner can be a great gift to someone who is trying to listen to the inner teacher.

With five minutes remaining in this two-hour process, a committee member needs to say, "It's time for affirmations and celebrations." I have served on many clearness committees, and I have never known these final five minutes to be a false or forced exercise. As the process comes to an end, I almost always realize that I have just seen with my own eyes something amazing and precious: the reality and power of the human soul. I have watched a human being gain important and often unexpected insights from his or her inner teacher. In our kind of world, where the soul is so often shouted down, a chance to welcome it, honor it, and watch it do its work is clearly cause for celebration.

The soul work that goes on in a clearness committee is quiet, subtle, and nearly impossible to put into words. But let the following words from one participant testify to the way the process can give tangible form to the most intangible of emotions:

> The question I have asked myself on so many different levels over the years is "How do I love _____?" The blank space could be filled in with a variety of words—my wife, my

children, my parents, my students, my fellow human beings.
. . . This has proven to be the most challenging question.

Recently, through my work [in a circle of trust], I gained new insight into this matter. As part of [our time together], we explored and took part in a clearness committee. In this process, I learned a new and most demanding way to listen, a way unencumbered by my own antipathies and judgments. I learned to listen openly for the soul of another, for that which is genuine and sacred.

In a moment of realization, I saw that this was the way I could put love into practice—by listening selflessly with complete attention to another. I could do this at any time with anyone I met. I could simply practice love through listening. Suddenly the most evasive, idealistic notion came softly down to earth.[2]

A Bird in the Hand

We are all shaped by conventional culture. So we all come into a clearness committee carrying a gravitational force that tries to pull our relationships back to fixing, saving, advising, and setting each other straight.

To help people resist this pull, members of a clearness committee are asked to follow behavioral rules so specific that they can seem ludicrous. Do not hand the focus person a tissue if he or she cries; do not laugh aloud if he or she cracks a joke; maintain a neutral expression when speaking and listening; allow the focus person to refrain from making eye contact for two full hours.

When I teach these ground rules, people often say that they feel intimidated by this level of "micromanagement." My response, I confess, is "Good!" When we agree to hold someone's soul in trust, we need to feel the weight of that commitment in order to do the job well. And people who teach others this process need to raise the behavioral bar so high that it will be too embarrassing for anyone to break the rules casually, minimizing the chance that a focus person will be harmed.

Appendix C

But as we raise the bar, we run the risk of turning the clearness committee into a process driven more by law than by the spirit of the law. If we are to make this space safe for the soul, a spirit of hospitality is at least as important as rules that help us act hospitably.

So in addition to teaching the rules, I offer people two clear and simple images that suggest the spirit behind the rules. I offer the first image *before* I teach the rules that have been laid out in this chapter: as members of a clearness committee, we are to create and protect a space to be occupied *only* by the focus person. For two hours, we are to act as if we had no reason for existing except to hold the focus person in a safe space, giving him or her our undivided attention, and guarding the borders of that space against anything that might distract that person.

The rules that guide our behavior are designed to keep us from invading that space, from saying or doing anything that would draw attention toward ourselves. That is why we cannot explain ourselves when the focus person objects to a question or offer comfort when the focus person cries or interpret the focus person's nonverbal speech. Behaviors like these put our needs and agendas into the space, displacing the focus person's soul.

The image of "creating and protecting a space" where we can attend exclusively to the focus person answers almost every question about the conduct of a clearness committee. Should I take notes as the focus person speaks? If note-taking distracts me from attending to the focus person, the answer is no; if note-taking helps me pay attention, the answer is yes. What if the focus person or a member of the committee needs to use the bathroom? The focus person will leave with a brief explanation, and members will maintain silence until he or she returns; a committee member will leave quietly, without explanation, while the process continues and will return to the circle as quietly as he or she left.

There is one more rule that helps us hold safe space for the focus person—the rule of "double confidentiality." Once the committee ends, nothing said in it will ever be repeated to anyone. People who took notes during the meeting must give them to the focus person before they leave. This not only guarantees confidentiality, but it also leaves the focus person with a great gift: a detailed record of what his or her soul was saying when it felt safe enough to tell the truth.

The second part of double confidentiality is as important as the first: committee members are forbidden from approaching the focus person a day, a week, or a year later, saying, "Remember when you said such-and-such? Well, I have a thought to share with you about that." The focus person may seek one of us out for further exploration. But if we were to pursue that person with our feedback or advice, we would violate his or her solitude. Focus persons often say that of all the clearness committee rules, double confidentiality's the one that gives them the most confidence that in this space they can speak their truth freely.

After I have taught the rules, and just before the committee process begins, I offer a second image, an image many have found helpful. For the next two hours, I suggest, we are to hold the soul of the focus person as if we were holding a small bird in the palms of our two hands.

As we do so, we are likely to experience three temptations, and it is important that we resist all of them:

• After a while, our hands may start to close around the bird, wanting to take this creature apart and find out what makes it tick. Resist this temptation: our job is not to analyze but simply to hold in open trust.

• As the time goes by, our arms may begin to tire, and we may find ourselves tempted to lay the bird down: attention flags, the mind wanders, and we are no longer holding the focus person at the center of our awareness. We must resist this temptation too. A bird is light, and a soul is even lighter. If we understand that we are under no obligation to fix, save, advise, or set this person straight, our burden will disappear, and we can hold this soul for two hours without tiring.

• Toward the end of the process—having held the bird openly with the best of intentions—we may find our cupped hands making a subtle but persistent upward motion, encouraging the bird to fly: "Don't you see what you have learned here? Aren't you ready to take off, to act on what you now know?" Resist this temptation

APPENDIX C

too. This bird will fly when it is ready, and we cannot possibly know when that will be.

The success of a clearness committee does not depend on whether the focus person "solves" his or her problem and is ready to act. Life, as everyone knows, does not unfold so neatly. The success of a clearness committee depends simply on whether we have held the focus person safely, for two full hours, in our open hands. When we do, the focus person almost always receives new insights from the inner teacher—and often a revelation or two.

When the clearness committee is finished, we do not need to stop holding the focus person. As the group disbands, the image that often comes to me is that of drawing my open hands into my open heart, where I can continue to hold the focus person in my thoughts, my caring, and my prayers.

I have taught this way of "being alone together" to thousands of people over the past thirty years. When the process ends, I always ask, "When was the last time a small group of caring, competent adults held you at the center of their attention for two full hours with nothing on their minds except creating and protecting space where you could hear your soul speak?" With rare exceptions, I have heard only one answer: "Never in my life have I experienced anything like this. "

There are many good ways to be together—life would be quite dreadful if all our interactions were governed by clearness committee rules! Still, it seems a great shame that we spend so much time within easy reach of each other and rarely, if ever, extend this kind of support for each other's inner journey.

But it is never too late. Virginia Shorey was a gifted high school teacher—and an extraordinary human being—who sought and received such support in the final months of her life. A participant in a two-year circle of trust, she learned after the group began that she had incurable cancer; she died before the group ended.

The people in Virginia's circle were companions on her journey, and beneficiaries of her great courage, in part through four clearness committees that Virginia requested and wrote about in her journal:[3]

Everyone [in these clearness committees] asked me very honest and compassionate questions. I opened myself up to them, my fears, and all the emotions I could not describe. I bared my intentions, my unfinished goals, dreams, and the fear of my life ending so soon, and also my fears for my family. I told them about how I am not through learning and giving yet. I wanted to write a book but now my world was crumbling. My committee did not comfort me. Neither did they fix me. I felt very safe around them. I found strength in their presence. After these [sessions], I began to understand my illness, and even accepted it as a gift. These clearness committees were my allies in getting out of my own jungle.

Shortly before Virginia died, she wrote me to express her gratitude not only for her clearness committees but for her entire circle of trust. I cannot imagine better words with which to close this chapter:

The reason I'm writing to you is the deep appreciation that I feel in my heart for [this circle]. It has blessed my life so much and has given me all sorts of insights, not only in my teaching but also in my personal and family life.

For one thing, it has given me true courage to respect and honor myself and thus paved new ways to really know myself. It helped me understand the paradoxes of life, especially when I was diagnosed with terminal cancer. It made me aware of my resources. . . . I've learned to see beyond my senses, to see the spiritual world through silence and meditation, through different eyes.

I've learned to appreciate nature like never before, the cycles, and the seasons. I've come to the point of seeing that others are worthy of my respect, and that I am also worthy of theirs.

Most of all, I learned that we are all a part of a larger community, and hence have tremendously altered my belief system. Because of [this circle], I've learned to conquer my fears and come to know that my resources are limitless.

Appendix C

Indeed, I've come to fully understand the courage to live and die and how magnificent it is to know true self!

NOTES

1. Setting up clearness committees in a circle of trust sometimes involves a little math. A circle of seven people or less can serve as a "committee of the whole" for one of its members. But circles of larger size need to have enough volunteers as focus persons so that everyone can be on a committee without any committee being too large or too small; for example, in a circle of seventeen, three volunteers are needed, and in a circle of twenty-four, four volunteers are needed. When clearness committees are formed in the context of a larger circle, committee members are assigned by the facilitator (rather than chosen by the focus person, as they are when a committee is formed apart from such a circle). Before making the assignments, the facilitator asks each focus person for two lists of names: people that he or she would especially like to have on the committee and people that he or she would not want to have on the committee. The facilitator assigns as many from the first list as possible and guarantees not to assign any from the second list.
2. I am grateful to Jack Petrash for giving me permission to use his words.
3. I am grateful to the late Virginia Shorey, a brave and inspiring woman, who sent me these words and gave me permission to use them. And I am grateful to her husband, Roscoe Shorey, who gave me permission to use her name here.

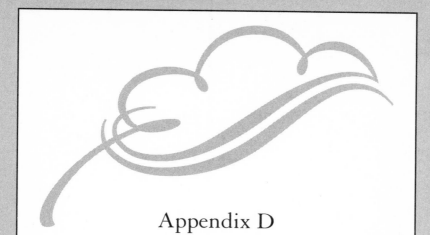

Appendix D

About the Center for Courage & Renewal

CENTER FOR
Courage & Renewal

RECONNECTING WHO YOU ARE WITH WHAT YOU DO

When we reconnect who we are with what we do,
we approach our lives and our work
with renewed passion, commitment, and integrity.

The Center for Courage & Renewal offers opportunities for individuals, professions, institutions, and communities to rekindle the heart's imperatives and rejoin them to the work we do. The Center prepares and supports Courage & Renewal facilitators who lead retreats and programs that foster personal renewal, professional integrity, and vocational clarity.

Since 1997, the Center has supported the development of Courage to Teach® retreats for educators and has contributed to the national discourse about education reform through the writings of Parker J. Palmer and others. What began as a quiet experiment to reclaim "the heart of the teacher" has grown into a significant movement promoting courage and renewal in leadership and life.

The Center has prepared nearly one hundred fifty facilitators through its Courage & Renewal Facilitator Preparation Program. These facilitators have in turn contributed to the personal and professional renewal of thousands of pre-K–12 teachers and school leaders across the United States and in Canada.

In addition to serving public school educators, who remain at the heart of the Center's mission, the Center's work has evoked great interest from persons in other arenas, including health care, religion, law, philanthropy, and the nonprofit sector. To reflect this expansion of its work, in 2005 the Center changed its name from the Center for Teacher Formation to the Center for Courage & Renewal, whose tagline, "Reconnecting who you are with what you do," expresses its abiding purpose.

In response to the expanded interest in its work—and energized by the enthusiastic reception given Parker J. Palmer's *A Hidden Wholeness: The Journey Toward an Undivided Life* (Jossey-Bass, 2004)—the Center now offers cross-professional "circle of trust" retreats. These retreats provide support for individuals in many walks of life who seek to live "divided no more." The Center's Web site offers links to programs and resources that will assist people in creating their own circles of trust, including access to Courage & Renewal facilitators who can consult with and/or lead such circles on a contractual basis.

Center for Courage & Renewal
321 High School Road NE, Suite D3, PMB 375
Bainbridge Island, WA 98110
(206) 855-9140
info@couragerenewal.org

To learn more, please visit our Web site at
www.CourageRenewal.org.

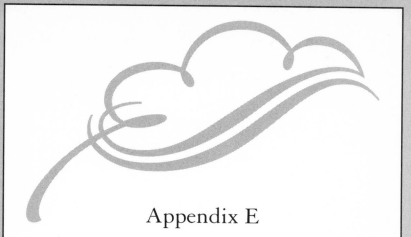

Appendix E

The Courage to Teach
A Retreat Program for
Personal Renewal and
Institutional Transformation

Reflections by Parker J. Palmer

In *The Courage to Teach,* I asked, "Is it possible to embody our best insights about teaching and learning in a social movement that might revitalize education?" (p. 169). Ten years later, I have an answer, and it is yes. Behind that answer are the committed and inspiring teachers and administrators I have met because of the book—educators who are coming together in community to cultivate the only source of power that cannot be taken from us, the power of the heart, the spirit, the soul.

Over the past decade, facilitators associated with the Center for Courage & Renewal (see Appendix D) have conducted countless Courage to Teach® retreats with teachers and administrators around the United States and in several places abroad. Through this work, we have learned that creating settings in which it is safe for educators to explore, alone and together, the "inner landscapes" of their lives has significant real-world outcomes:

- Students start experiencing their teachers as having greater authenticity. As teachers come to know their own hearts better, they are better able to see what is in their students' hearts, thus creating safe classroom spaces more conducive to learning.

- Collegial relations are strengthened, building a form of social capital called "relational trust" that we know is critical to a school's success in helping students learn.[1]

- As people come into firmer possession of their own hearts, they are more likely to take leadership roles, informal as well as formal, and their leadership is more likely to be life-giving for others.

- Personal and relational outcomes like these help people come together to create institutional policies and practices that strengthen the educational mission, contributing to the revitalization of our schools.

The fact that we can announce good news of this sort in the midst of very hard times—for our world, our country, and education itself—is primarily due, of course, to the teachers and administrators who are out there doing the heavy lifting. Those of us who have been involved in the Courage to Teach program feel both privileged and proud to have been providing support for some of these educators over the past fourteen years, support we intend to offer for many years to come.

THE COURAGE TO TEACH PROGRAM

The Courage to Teach® (CTT) is a program of quarterly retreats for the personal and professional renewal of educators, originally designed for pre-K–12 teachers, counselors, and administrators on whom our society depends for so much but for whom we provide so little. The CTT program focuses exclusively on renewing educators' inner lives, knowing that when we do so, their transformations will spill over into transformed relationships and institutions.

The Courage to Teach program . . .

- Renews heart, mind, and spirit through an exploration of the inner landscape of a teacher's life
- Reconnects one's professional role to one's identity and integrity, identifying and honoring gifts and strengths and acknowledging limits
- Creates a context for careful listening and deep connection that honors diversity in persons and professions
- Helps educators create safe spaces and trusting relationships in their schools and their communities
- Generates inner-life energies in teachers and students alike that can contribute to the renewal of public education

---

 SEGMENT 22: TAKING HEART

To hear more about how the Courage to Teach program enables teachers to take heart so they can in turn give heart to their students, view Segment 22 on the DVD that accompanies this *Guide*.

Origins of the Program

The Courage to Teach program was launched in 1994 by the Fetzer Institute. I worked with Fetzer in pioneering an approach to the personal and professional renewal of educators that we then called "teacher formation." Here, educators are given a chance to reclaim wholeness and vocational clarity by listening to their "inner teacher" and making personal connections between their renewed spirits, the roles they play at work, and the revitalization of the institutions in which they work.

In 1997, the Center for Teacher Formation was established to expand and develop Courage to Teach programs across the country through the training, mentoring, and support of skilled retreat facilitators. In 2005, the Center for Teacher Formation changed its name to the Center for Courage & Renewal in response to calls from many people in fields other than education—including health care, religious life, law, philanthropy, and the nonprofit sector. As part of this expanded mission, the language of "teacher formation" was replaced by the concept of working in "circles of trust."[2]

What Happens at Courage to Teach Retreats?

Each CTT group consists of twenty to thirty educators who gather for a three-day facilitated retreat each quarter over a one- to two-year period. In circles of trust that involve large-group, small-group, and solitary opportunities, they explore "the heart of a teacher," using personal stories, reflection on classroom practice, and insights from poets, storytellers, and various wisdom traditions to aid and abet the process.

Each retreat follows themes related to the season in which it is held, using the rich metaphors of the cycle of nature as ways of exploring vocational and other inner-life questions. For example, the fall theme, "The Seed of True Self," provides a rubric under which people can revisit the passions, experiences, gifts, or values that drew them into teaching in the first place and reflect on how their educational journey has unfolded. The winter themes of darkness and death, dormancy and renewal, provide a context to talk about seasons of grief and loss in our work and in our lives. Spring offers the paradox of new life emerging from winter's real and apparent losses, while summer is a season in which to reflect on fruition, abundance, and the harvest of one's work in the feeding of others.

About Courage & Renewal Facilitators

Skilled facilitators are at the heart of the Courage to Teach program. They are our primary means of quality control, a notion we must and do take very seriously in a program that promises safety for the soul. These facilitators have been carefully prepared by the Center for Courage & Renewal to create trustworthy spaces in which participants can explore their inner lives, professional practice, and related issues and dilemmas. Courage & Renewal facilitators come from a variety of backgrounds: some are pre-K–12 educators, some are teacher educators, and some have organizational development or other human service backgrounds.

 SEGMENT 23: THE FOUR SEASONS

To learn more about the use of seasonal images and metaphors to frame an inner journey, view Segment 23 on the DVD that accompanies this *Guide*.

THE COURAGE TO TEACH AND
INSTITUTIONAL TRANSFORMATION

What kind of leverage can a retreat-based program that works with "the inner life" have on education at large? A great deal, as the experience of the past decade and more has shown. In the Afterword to the tenth anniversary edition of *The Courage to Teach,* I offer evidence of this impact in the form of conferences held; research conducted; widespread publication of articles, journals, and books; and innovative programs in education, medicine, and other fields where people have challenged their institutions to change.

Why has CTT been so successful and had such a broad impact? The answer, in part, is that it meets a deeply felt need among teachers and other professionals for meaningful inner work and generative communal connections that few professional development programs provide.

But I believe that the success of CTT also reflects our adherence to a developmental strategy that flows from our "movement model" of social change. This model begins with individuals who make a decision to live "divided no more" (the "Rosa Parks decision") and eventuates in incremental institutional change driven by communities of people who constellate around the core values of identity and integrity. The model also posits that powerful ideas—well articulated and embodied with discipline and integrity over time—can develop lives of their own and multiply in ways that we can neither predict nor control.

A movement is most likely to succeed when it attends to both the microcosm and the macrocosm, cultivating individuals and small-scale communities who can make a difference in local settings, as well as large-scale conversations that help people find the language and legitimation for advocating change.

The Center for Courage & Renewal has made meaningful contributions on both of these fronts. Supported by Courage to Teach retreats and other circle of trust programs, many individuals have been able to reclaim their professional hearts. Supported by a number of books and articles related to the Center that contribute to the national discourse on education reform, a growing number of people (including many in leadership roles) have been empowered to go public with a vision for reclaiming vocational vitality in the professions.

As I wrote toward the end of *The Courage to Teach* (pp. 189–190):

> I am a teacher at heart, and I am not naturally drawn to the
> rough-and-tumble of social change. I would sooner teach
> than spend my energies helping a movement along and
> taking the hits that come with it. Yet if I care about teaching,
> I must care not only for my students and my subject but also
> for the conditions, inner and outer, that bear on the work
> teachers do. Finding a place in the movement for educational
> reform is one way to exercise that larger caring. . . .

As we find our place in the movement, we will discover that there is no essential conflict between loving to teach and working to reform education.

The accompanying box provides a sketch of the movement model. Chapter VII in *The Courage to Teach* offers an extended discussion of the model and its implication for education, and the Afterword to the tenth anniversary edition focuses the model on the "education of a new professional."

The Four Stages of Social Change

Stage 1: Divided No More
- Isolated individuals reach a point where the gap between their inner and outer lives becomes so painful that they resolve to live "divided no more."
- These people may leave or remain within institutions—but they abandon the logic of institutions and find an alternative center for their lives.
- These people do not hate institutions—they love them too much to allow them to sink to their lowest form.
- The logic of punishment is transformed: no punishment can be greater than conspiring in one's own diminishment.

Stage 2: Communities of Congruence
- Isolated individuals discover each other in groups that develop around declarations of personal need and operate by alternative ground rules.
- These groups sustain people's sense of sanity in a world where the divided life is regarded as safe and sane.
- These groups give an experience of leadership and efficacy to people who have been denied that opportunity.
- These groups practice a fragile private language so it can grow strong enough to enter the rough-and-tumble public realm.

Stage 3: Going Public

- Empowered by communities of congruence, movement advocates find their public voice.
- Movement words, images, and symbols become more visible, and converts are gained.
- Critics are also gained—the movement is scrutinized and critiqued and must be clarified and refined.
- Leaders within communities of congruence become public leaders.

Stage 4: Alternative Rewards

- Movements develop—and become—alternative reward systems, thus relativizing the sanctions that are the basis of every institution's power.
- Some of the alternative rewards are external (jobs, income, status, visibility, colleagues), and some are internal (a sense of identity and integrity).
- The logic of rewards is transformed: no reward can be greater than living "divided no more."
- The energies that began in abandoning the logic of institutions come full circle to alter the logic of institutions.

ABOUT THE
COURAGE TO TEACH PROGRAM

Please view the DVD segment titled "About the Courage to Teach Program," which provides general information and personal stories about the impact of the Courage to Teach program on individual teachers and education reform.

NOTES

1. See Anthony Bryk and Barbara Schneider, *Trust in Schools: A Core Resource for Improvement* (New York: Russell Sage Foundation, 2004).
2. For more on circles of trust, see Parker J. Palmer, *A Hidden Wholeness: The Journey Toward an Undivided Life* (San Francisco: Jossey-Bass, 2004).

Appendix F

Resources for
Courage to Teach
Discussion Groups

T his list includes resources relevant to professionals not only in education but also in other fields.

PRIMARY RESOURCES

A Hidden Wholeness: The Journey Toward an Undivided Life, by Parker J. Palmer (San Francisco: Jossey-Bass, 2004).

This book addresses four compelling themes: the shape of an integral life; the meaning of community; teaching and learning for transformation; and nonviolent social change. In the opening chapters, Palmer explores what it means to live an undivided life, one where our inner truth can find expression and value in our outer lives, despite the pressures we may face. In the remaining chapters, he articulates with great care the conditions necessary to create circles of trust, outlining in considerable detail the approach used by the Center for Courage & Renewal in retreats with educators and professionals in other fields. He then offers a model of community, based on the principles and practices of formation that can help us embrace nonviolence in the workplace.

Living the Questions: Essays Inspired by the Work and Life of Parker J. Palmer, edited by Sam M. Intrator (San Francisco: Jossey-Bass, 2005).

This book explores the dynamic interplay between the inner life of spirit and the outer life of work. The equally distinguished contributors, who come from a wide range of professions—university presidents, scientists, physicians, religious leaders, business consultants, public school educators, philanthropists, and community organizers—bear witness to the depth, breadth, and reach of Palmer's work. These intimate essays and stories shed new light on some of the most important topics of our time: living an integral life, teaching and learning for transformation, creating community, and contributing to nonviolent social change. (See the accompanying box.)

USING *LIVING THE QUESTIONS*

The essays in *Living the Questions* are short, accessible pieces that can help "create a space" and frame a good conversation in small groups for a wide variety of professions. As one of the authors, David Dodson, president of Make a Difference in Communities, writes:

> Palmer has become an indispensable resource for legions of people working for community change. Whether the goal is better schools, safer neighborhoods, or more transparent government, Palmer's ideas have an uncanny ability to make us better advocates and leaders. He calls us to our conscience, pricks our hypocrisy, and stiffens our spines. By transforming those who would lead, his ideas help leaders transform their settings.

We especially recommend the following essays for those who are not pre-K–12 educators but would like to pursue the basic themes of *The Courage to Teach* in their own professions:

Medical educators would be interested in learning about the connections between the "Courage to Teach" program and medical education and healing programs for physicians as described in Henry Emmon's "Insights on the Inner Life of Healers" and Paul Batalden and David Leach's "The Inner and Outer Life in Medicine: Honoring Values, Relationships, and the Human Element in Physicians' Lives."

Higher education leaders would enjoy Jay Casbon's "Turning Toward a New Leadership"; Douglas Orr's "A Journey of the Heart: Seeking the Questions Worth Living"; and Diana Chapman Walsh's "On Beyond Revenge: Leadership for Peace."

Foundation executives and philanthropists would be attuned to many of the issues raised in Michael Lerner's "On Philanthropy and the Inner Life."

Clergy would welcome David Maitland's "Late Openings?"

Teacher educators would be interested in the models explored by Sally Z. Hare in her essay "The Lehrergarten: A Vision for Teacher Education."

Organizational and community development leaders would find much to offer in David Dodson's "Inspiring Communities of Caring and Conscience"; Russ S. Moxley's "It Also Takes Courage to Lead"; Peter M. Senge's "A World Shaped by Choice"; and Margaret Wheatley's "The True Professional."

Courage & Renewal facilitators would take interest in Marcy Jackson and Rick Jackson's "The Threads We Follow"; Marianne Novak Houston's "Learning by Heart: An Ode to My Vocation as a Teacher"; and Chip Wood's "Notions of Presence."

Political leaders would value Doug Tanner's "Soul and Role, Politicians and Politics."

Business leaders would be interested to know of the connection between Palmer's work and business as described by L. J. Rittenhouse in her essay "If We Pay Attention."

Let Your Life Speak: Listening for the Voice of Vocation, by Parker J.
Palmer (San Francisco: Jossey-Bass, 2000).

This book invites us to listen to our inner teacher and follow its lead toward a sense of meaning and purpose. Telling stories from his own life and the lives of others who have made a difference, Palmer shares insights gained from darkness and depression as well as fulfillment and joy, illuminating a pathway toward vocation for all who seek the true calling of their lives.

Chapter V is the latest version of one of Palmer's best-known essays, "Leading from Within." Here Palmer defines a leader as "someone with the power to project either shadow or light upon some part of the world, and upon the lives of the people who dwell there. A leader shapes the ethos in which others must live, an ethos as light-filled as heaven or as shadowy as hell. A *good* leader has high awareness of the interplay of inner shadow and light, lest the act of leadership do more harm than good." He challenges leaders to become aware of, and self-correcting about, those ways in which we project more shadow than light.

Stories of the Courage to Teach: Honoring the Teacher's Heart, edited by
Sam M. Intrator (San Francisco: Jossey-Bass, 2002).

This book is a collection of essays—written by teachers at every level of practice—that honors the hearts of all teachers who struggle to reconnect with the source of their vocation. These teachers have found ways to serve their students, rekindle their passion for teaching, connect in life-sustaining ways with colleagues, and work toward creating educational institutions that seek to be places that, as Palmer writes, "bring more light and life into the world." Their warm, practical, funny, and wise stories will provide inspiration, companionship, and hope to teachers who strive to reclaim the courage to teach.

Among the many excellent essays, you may be particularly interested in Robert Kraft's "Teaching Excellence and the Inner Life of a Faculty" (on using CTT with college faculty); Kirstin Tonningsen's "Reclaiming Identity: Sharing a Teacher's Truth" (on her CTT retreat experience), and Elizabeth Keats Flores's "Of Aliens and Space" (on using *The Courage to Teach Guide for Reflection and Renewal* in her college classes). The book also contains a Foreword and an extensive Afterword by Parker J. Palmer.

"The Politics of the Brokenhearted," by Parker J. Palmer, in *Deepening the American Dream: Reflections on the Inner Life and Spirit of Democracy,* edited by Mark Nepo (San Francisco: Jossey-Bass, 2005).

This collection of essays explores the inner life of democracy, and the spiritual dimensions of the American dream of life, liberty, and the pursuit of happiness. Of special interest to readers of *The Courage to Teach Guide for Reflection and Renewal* is the essay by Parker J. Palmer, "The Politics of the Brokenhearted," in which he explores the theme of holding tensions that "break our hearts"—break them either apart or open—a theme relevant not only to civic life but to education and many other arenas of work. In September 2005, at a public forum on *Deepening the American Dream* held at the National Press Club in Washington, D.C., Palmer gave a talk based on this essay, which can be found at www.fetzer.org/PDF/DAD_Selections_from_the_Public _Forum.pdf.

Leading from Within: Poetry That Sustains the Courage to Lead, edited by Sam M. Intrator and Megan Scribner (San Francisco: Jossey-Bass, 2007).

This collection of ninety-three poems—by such poets as Mary Oliver, Langston Hughes, Wendell Berry, Naomi Shihab Nye, William Stafford, and T. S. Eliot—will touch the minds and hearts of leaders and encourage and sustain them in their work. Each poem is accompanied by a brief reflection from the leader who chose it, explaining the significance of the poem in his or her life and work. There is inspiration here for leaders of all kinds, in any setting. Parker J. Palmer's Introduction is a thoughtful exploration of issues in leadership.

Teaching with Fire: Poetry That Sustains the Courage to Teach, edited by Sam M. Intrator and Megan Scribner (San Francisco: Jossey-Bass, 2003).

Those of us who care about the young and their education must find ways to remember what teaching and learning are really about. We must find ways to keep our hearts alive as we serve our students. Poetry has the power to keep us vital and focused on what really matters in life and in schooling. This book is a wonderful collection of eighty-eight poems from such well-loved poets as Walt Whitman, Langston Hughes, Billy Collins, Emily Dickinson, and Pablo Neruda. Each of these evocative poems is accompanied by a brief story from an educator explaining the significance of the poem in his or her life's work. The book also includes an essay that describes how poetry can be used to grow both personally and professionally, and a compelling Introduction by Parker J. Palmer and Tom Vander Ark.

A Reader's Guide for Teaching with Fire, compiled by Megan Scribner (2005).

This guide is a compendium of ideas on how to use poetry to inspire, teach, work with others, and create community. A free copy of this guide is available at www.CourageRenewal.org.

OTHER WORKS BY PARKER J. PALMER

The following resources can be downloaded from the Web site of the Center for Courage & Renewal (www.CourageRenewal.org) under "Related Resources/Related Writings."

Print Resources

"Community, Conflict, and Ways of Knowing," by Parker J. Palmer, *Change,* Sept.-Oct. 1987.

"Community is not opposed to conflict. On the contrary, community is precisely that place where an arena for creative conflict is protected by the compassionate fabric of human caring itself. If you ask what holds community together, what makes this capacity for relatedness possible, the only honest answer I can give brings me to that dangerous realm called the spiritual. The only answer I can give is that what makes community possible is love."

"Divided No More," by Parker J. Palmer, *Change,* Mar.-Apr. 1992.

Parker Palmer explores a movement approach to educational reform. He writes that the genius of movements is paradoxical: they abandon the logic of organizations in order to gather the power necessary to rewrite the logic of organizations. He explores four definable stages in the movements he has studied. By understanding these stages, we may come to see that we are engaged in a movement today, that we hold power in our hands—a form of power that has driven real change in human history.

"Evoking the Spirit in Public Education," by Parker J. Palmer, *Educational Leadership,* Dec. 1998–Jan. 1999.

"As a teacher, I have seen the price we pay for a system of education so fearful of things spiritual that it fails to address the real issues of our lives—dispensing facts at the expense of meaning, information at the expense of wisdom. The price is a school system that alienates and dulls us, that graduates young people who have had no mentoring in the questions that both enliven and vex the human spirit."

"Good Talk About Good Teaching: Improving Teaching Through Conversation and Community," by Parker J. Palmer, *Change,* Nov.-Dec. 1993.

"From the myriad topics that emerge once one starts looking deeper than technique, I want to describe four that I have found effective in my work with faculty:

- Critical moments in teaching and learning
- The human condition of teachers and learners
- Metaphors and images of what we are doing when we teach
- Autobiographical reflection on the great teachers who helped bring us into academic life."

"Good Teaching," by Parker J. Palmer, *Change,* Jan.-Feb. 1990.

"Good teaching is an act of generosity, a whim of the wanton muse, a craft that may grow with practice, and always risky business. It is, to speak plainly, a maddening mystery. How can I explain the wild variety of teachers who have incited me to learn—from one whose lectures were tropical downpours that drowned out most other comments, to one who created an arid silence by walking into class and asking, 'Any questions?'"

"The Grace of Great Things," by Parker J. Palmer, in *The Heart of Learning: Spirituality in Education,* edited by Steven Glazer (New York: Tarcher/Putnam, 1999), pp. 15–32.

If we could reclaim our sense of the sacred in education—defined as that to which we owe respect—how would it transform our knowing, teaching, and learning? Parker Palmer explores ways to recover the humility that makes authentic education possible.

"The Heart of a Teacher," by Parker J. Palmer, *Change,* Nov.-Dec. 1997.

"Teaching, like any truly human activity, emerges from one's inwardness, for better or worse. As I teach, I project the condition of my soul onto my students, my subject, and our way of being together. The entanglements I experience in the classroom are often no more or less than the convolutions of my inner life. Viewed from this angle, teaching holds a mirror to the soul. If I am willing to look in that mirror, and not run from what I see, I have a chance to gain self-knowledge—and knowing myself is as crucial to good teaching as knowing my students and my subject."

"Leadership and the Inner Journey: An Interview with Parker Palmer," by L. J. Rittenhouse, *Leader to Leader,* Fall, 2001.

Parker Palmer has inspired a national movement to reform teaching and education. Here, in conversation with L. J. Rittenhouse, an executive consultant who tracks the connection between CEO language and financial performance, Palmer explains why the inner journey is a prerequisite to authentic leadership.

"Reflections on a Program for the 'Formation of Teachers,'" by Parker J. Palmer (Kalamazoo, Mich.: Fetzer Institute, 1992).

In this Fetzer Institute occasional paper, Parker Palmer first sketched the conceptual foundations of what was soon to become the Courage to Teach program. Palmer asks, "How can we move from this conviction about the soul-sources of good teaching into a program for the formation of teachers? The missing link is a perceptive diagnosis of how and why teachers lose their souls. What are the factors that obscure or distort the identity and integrity of the teacher so that he or she is not teaching *from* personal wholeness and, therefore, cannot possibly teach *toward* personal wholeness?"

"Teaching with Heart and Soul: Reflections on Spirituality in Teacher Education," by Parker J. Palmer, *Journal of Teacher Education,* Nov.-Dec. 2003.

This article revolves around two questions: Is there a "spiritual" dimension to good teaching? And if so, do spiritual considerations have a place in teacher education? Defining spirituality as "the eternal human yearning to be connected with something larger than our own egos,"

Palmer answers both questions in the affirmative, and he explores the implications of these answers for teacher education. The article pays special attention to a "pedagogy of the soul" that respects both cultural diversity and the separation of church and state and is relevant to institutional and social change as well as personal transformation.

"The Soul in Depression," an interview with Parker J. Palmer on National Public Radio's *Speaking of Faith*.

Hosted by Krista Tippett, *Speaking of Faith* is National Public Radio's weekly conversation about religion, meaning, ethics, and ideas, produced and distributed by American Public Media. Week after week, it grapples with themes of American life—asking how perspectives of faith might distinctively inform and illuminate our public reflection. This particular program on the experience of depression, including Palmer's personal journey with it, is available as both an audio file and a transcript of the interview at www.speakingoffaith.publicradio.org/programs/depression/index.shtml.

Audiovisual Media Resources

"Leading from Within: Reclaiming Selfhood in Professional Life," a lecture given by Parker J. Palmer at Wellesley College.

Video of this October 26, 2005, lecture is available online through the WGBH Forum Network at www.forum-network.org/wgbh/forum. php?lecture_id=2047.

"Thomas Merton's Asian Journey," an interview with Parker J. Palmer on Wisconsin Public Radio's *Here on Earth: Radio Without Borders*.

Parker Palmer and host Jean Feraca explore Thomas Merton's journey from the traditional Roman Catholicism of a devout young Trappist monk into a more mature and expansive version of Christianity in respectful dialogue with Eastern spirituality. Available at www.wpr.org/hereonearth/ archive_070131k.cfm.

"The Violence of Our Knowledge: Toward a Spirituality of Higher Education," by Parker J. Palmer. Seventh Annual Michael Keenan Memorial Lecture, St. Thomas More College, University of Saskatchewan, Saskatoon.

This 1993 address is available from the 21st Century Learning Initiative at www.21learn.org/arch/articles/palmer_spirituality.html.

ADDITIONAL RESOURCES

Listed below are books and journals by people connected with the Courage to Teach program which provide additional perspectives that we believe you will find inspiring and helpful.

"Courage to Teach," by Scott Driscoll, *Horizon Magazine,* Sept. 2005.

This article describes a "Courage to Teach" program in Washington State, following a group of teachers both in retreat and back in the classroom.

"The Heart of a Teacher: Making the Connection Between Teaching and Inner Life," by Sam M. Intrator.

Sam Intrator gave this keynote speech about the "Courage to Teach" program in November 2004 at the tenth anniversary meeting of the International Step by Step Association in Budapest, Hungary.

Leadership and Spirit: Breathing New Vitality and Energy into Individuals and Organizations, by Russ S. Moxley (San Francisco: Jossey-Bass, 2000).

Russ Moxley, leadership consultant and Courage & Renewal facilitator, shows leaders at all levels how they can link leadership and spirit to generate a more vibrant and essential brand of leadership, one that promotes the creativity, vitality, and well-being of others.

"The Person in the Profession: Renewing Teacher Vitality Through Professional Development," by Sam M. Intrator and Robert Kunzman, *Educational Forum,* Fall 2006.

A teacher's vocational vitality, or capacity to be present and deeply connected to his or her students, is not a fixed, indelible condition but a state that ebbs and flows with the context and challenges of the teaching life. In light of this, an emerging form of professional development programming explicitly devoted to nourishing the inner life or core dimensions of teachers is increasingly important for today's educators.

"Rediscovering the Call to Teach: A New Vision for Professional and Personal Development," by Caryl Hurtig Casbon, Ruth Shagoury, and Gregory A. Smith, *Language Arts,* May 2005.

The authors of this article argue that professional development on literacy instruction should go beyond instructional methods to teacher identity. Reading and discussing poetry and literature, as well as writing to examine powerful themes in teachers' lives, can help educators explore and deepen their identity as language arts teachers. The authors describe a two-year personal and professional development model based on the work of Parker Palmer called the "Courage to Teach." Interviews and surveys with participants show that the retreat setting, seasonal themes, and communal interaction have a profound effect on teachers' and administrators' renewed commitment to literacy education.

"Starting with Soul," by Sam M. Intrator and Robert Kunzman, *Educational Leadership,* Mar. 2006.

This article describes why rekindling teachers' deep sense of purpose is not a luxury but a necessity if teachers are to do their best and most inspired work.

Teaching, Learning, and Loving: Reclaiming Passion in Educational Practice, edited by Daniel P. Liston and James W. Garrison (New York: Routledge Falmer, 2004).

The emotional features of teaching and learning, while crucial in everyday classroom practice, are all too often overlooked by theorists and educational researchers. This book brings together a group of prominent scholars whose work explores, among other things, the connections between reason and emotion in teaching and learning. Daniel Liston, an educator and Courage & Renewal facilitator, James Garrison, and their collaborators stress the importance of engaging in more conversations about the emotional investments of teaching, the hazards they can present to teachers and students, and the losses teachers experience daily in their classrooms. In the process, the authors of this provocative collection reinvigorate the desire to create hope, meaning, and more effective teacher education.

Time to Teach, Time to Learn: Changing the Pace of School, by Chip
  Wood (Greenfield, Mass.: Northeast Foundation for Children,
  1999).

In this book, Chip Wood, cofounder of Northeast Foundation for
Children, and a Courage to Teach facilitator, confronts the epidemic
of "busyness" in our nation's K–8 schools. He offers teachers and administrators meaningful ways to change the quality of teaching and
learning for all children by changing our assumptions about time.

Tuned In and Fired Up, by Sam M. Intrator (New Haven, Conn.: Yale
  University Press, 2003).

In this compelling book, Sam Intrator analyzes powerful learning moments in a high school classroom. He offers five detailed case study
portraits of these experiences, describing in each case how the teacher
shaped the culture of the class, made critical pedagogical decisions, and
connected students to the subject matter. By animating students to tap
into their creative strengths, inner resources, and natural enthusiasm,
Intrator shows how a teacher can engage students more deeply.

The Wounded Leader: How Real Leadership Emerges in Times of Crisis,
  by Richard H. Ackerman and Pat Maslin-Ostrowski (San
  Francisco: Jossey-Bass, 2002).

As any school principal or administrator can testify, the responsibilities of school leadership can take a leader from an inspired moment to
crisis in an instant. In this book, leaders share their stories and their
struggle to make sense of their wounding experiences. Ultimately, the
wounds become a gateway to healing and tremendous growth and
learning.

The Authors

PARKER J. PALMER is a highly respected writer, teacher, and activist who focuses on issues in education, community, leadership, spirituality, and social change. His work speaks deeply to people in many walks of life, including public schools, colleges and universities, religious institutions, corporations, foundations, and grassroots organizations.

Palmer served for fifteen years as senior associate of the American Association of Higher Education. He now serves as senior adviser to the Fetzer Institute. He founded the Center for Courage & Renewal (www.CourageRenewal.org), which oversees the Courage to Teach program for pre-K–12 educators across the country and parallel programs for people in other professions, including medicine, law, ministry, and philanthropy.

He has published a dozen poems, more than one hundred essays, and seven books, including several best-selling and award-winning titles: *A Hidden Wholeness, Let Your Life Speak, The Courage to Teach, The Active Life, To Know as We Are Known, The Company of Strangers,* and *The Promise of Paradox.*

Palmer's work has been recognized with ten honorary doctorates, two Distinguished Achievement Awards from the

National Educational Press Association, an Award of Excellence from the Associated Church Press, and major grants from the Danforth Foundation, the Lilly Endowment, and the Fetzer Institute.

In 1993, Palmer won the national award of the Council of Independent Colleges for Outstanding Contributions to Higher Education.

In 1998, the Leadership Project, a national survey of ten thousand administrators and faculty, named Palmer one of the thirty "most influential senior leaders" in higher education and one of the ten key "agenda setters" of the 1990s: "He has inspired a generation of teachers and reformers with evocative visions of community, knowing, and spiritual wholeness."

In 2001, Carleton College gave Palmer the Distinguished Alumni Achievement Award. The following year, the Accreditation Council for Graduate Medical Education created the Parker J. Palmer Courage to Teach Award, given annually to the directors of ten medical residency programs that exemplify patient-centered professionalism in medical education. A year later, the American College Personnel Association named Palmer its Diamond Honoree for outstanding contributions to the field of student affairs.

In 2005, Jossey-Bass published *Living the Questions: Essays Inspired by the Work and Life of Parker J. Palmer,* written by notable practitioners in a variety of fields including medicine, law, philanthropy, politics, economic development, pre-K–12, and higher education.

Parker J. Palmer received his Ph.D. in sociology from the University of California at Berkeley. A member of the Religious Society of Friends (Quaker), he lives with his wife, Sharon Palmer, in Madison, Wisconsin.

MEGAN SCRIBNER is an editor and researcher who has documented and evaluated projects for nonprofits for the past twenty-six years. She is coeditor of *Leading from Within: Poetry That Sustains the Courage to Lead* and *Teaching with Fire: Poetry That Sustains the Courage to Teach* and editor of *Navigating the Terrain of Childhood: A Guidebook for Meaningful Parenting and Heartfelt Discipline.* She has edited discussion guides, such as the one published by the World Resource Institute to accompany the *Bill Moyers Reports: Earth on Edge* video. She also coedited *Transformations of Myth Through Time: An Anthology of Readings* and the *Joseph Campbell Transformations of Myth Through Time Study Guide* and coauthored the project's *Faculty and Administrator's Manual*.

In addition to her writing and editing, Scribner is an adviser to the Fetzer Institute and with Sam Intrator has evaluated a number of renewal and leadership programs.

Scribner received her master's degree in American studies from George Washington University. She lives with her husband, Bruce Kozarsky, and their two daughters, Anya and Maya, in Takoma Park, Maryland.

About the DVD

PARKER J. PALMER INTERVIEW

ABOUT THE COURAGE TO TEACH PROGRAM

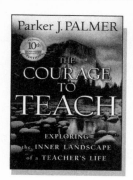

The Courage to Teach
Exploring the Inner Landscape of a Teacher's Life
10th Anniversary Edition
Parker J. Palmer

Hardcover/CD
ISBN: 978-0-7879-9686-4

"This book is for teachers who have good days and bad — and whose bad days bring the suffering that comes only from something one loves. It is for teachers who refuse to harden their hearts, because they love learners, learning, and the teaching life."

PARKER J. PALMER *[from the Introduction]*

In the tenth anniversary edition of his classic *The Courage to Teach*, Parker J. Palmer offers hope, encouragement, and guidance to teachers—and other professionals—who want to recover the heart of their vocation and calling. His new Foreword reflects on ten years of "courage work," which has spread beyond education to help teachers and other professionals recover meaning and depth in their work lives. And a new concluding chapter takes a fresh look at a new kind of professional and what it means to "take heart" in one's work.

BONUS: Includes an audio CD featuring a 45-minute conversation between Parker Palmer and his colleagues Marcy Jackson and Estrus Tucker from the Center for Courage & Renewal (www .CourageRenewal.org). They reflect on what they have learned from working with thousands of teachers in their "Courage to Teach" program and with others who yearn for greater integrity in their professional lives.

Parker J. Palmer is a highly respected writer, lecturer, teacher, and activist. His work speaks deeply to people from many walks of life, including public schools, college and universities, religious institutions, corporations, foundations, and grass-roots organizations. The Leadership Project, a 1998 survey of 10,000 American educators, named him one of the thirty most influential senior leaders in higher education and one of ten key "agenda-setters" of the past decade. Author of seven books—including the bestsellers *Let Your Life Speak* and *The Courage to Teach*—his writing has been recognized with ten honorary doctorates and several national awards. He holds a Ph.D. from the University of California at Berkeley and lives in Madison, Wisconsin.